City of Objects

City of Objects
Designs on Berlin
William Alsop Bruce McLean Jan Störmer

Texts and Pretexts
Mel Gooding

Demands of the Future
Bryan Appleyard

In 1991 Alsop and Störmer
was one of seventeen
practices invited to enter a
competition for the
reconstruction of the
Potsdamer Platz/Leipziger
Platz area of Berlin. This
book documents their
award-winning entry

The competition team:

William Alsop
Jonathan Adams
Stephen Biller
Jason Dickinson
Colin Foster
Adrian Friend
Holger Jaedicke
Isabelle Lousada
Bruce McLean
Ludwig Meyer
Benedict O'Looney

Model Makers:

William McLean
Carolyn Cloake
Camilla Wilkinson

Traffic Consultants:

Guy Battle
Chris McCarthy
Malcolm Fullard
at Ove Arup & Partners

First published 1992 by
Verlag für Architektur
Artemis & Winkler Verlag,
Zürich and Munich/
London Architectural Press

© Artemis Verlags AG Zürich
and William Alsop, 1992

ISBN 1 874056 25 0   (London)
ISBN 3 7608 8095 9   (Zürich)

British Library Cataloguing
in Publication Data

A CIP catalogue record
for this book is available
from the British Library

Set in Univers 55, 75 and
Monotype Baskerville

Imageset by Alphabet Set

Printed in Hong Kong

A London Architectural Press book

Publisher:
Tom Neville
Project Management:
Kasia Paveliev
Art Direction:
Jonathan Moberly
Design:
Borja Goyarrola
Photography:
Roderick Coyne
Captions:
James Allen
Jonathan Adams
Additional research:
Adrian Driscoll

The texts on pages 21 and 29
are by William Alsop.

The paintings are by
William Alsop, except those
on pages 26–27, 50–51,
66–67, and 82–83 which
are by William Alsop and
Bruce McLean.

Section and elevation
drawings are all reproduced
at a scale of 1:1400

Will Alsop and Bruce McLean first met at Riverside Studios, Hammersmith, in 1979. At the invitation of David Gothard Alsop had established a small office as 'architect in residence' in a back room overlooking the Thames, approached by an external metal spiral staircase. McLean was also working at Riverside, in a cramped, cupboard-like space, higher than wide. Alsop was preparing designs for the development of Riverside Studios; McLean making brilliantly coloured 'drawings' towards *The Masterwork, Award Winning Fishknife*, a large-scale 'performance sculpture' satirising the grandiose mediocrity of much modern architecture, and its debasement of modernist ideals: 'Nothing outside the rules. Liberty through conformity.'

Their creative conversation began there, with its recurrent focus upon the processes of art and architecture in their relation to the behaviour of people in the spaces where they live. In 1985, in a collaborative venture with McLean and Mel Gooding, Alsop drew up designs for a grand palace of arts, a place to work, play, experiment and pose, to be created out of a disused brewery silo in Mortlake. It was in that year that he made his first large-scale paintings, working alongside McLean in the studio. Since that date they have met regularly, convivially discussing architecture, art and life in general, and various projects in particular.

The most intensive of their collaborative exchanges took place in 1991 in the initial preparations for the proposals documented in this book. After many discussions in London about the Berlin project, Alsop joined McLean at his studio in Menorca for a week in July. There they worked together, developing, through drawing and painting, the principal ideas that were to animate the final scheme: of the street as object; of the adjoining squares as a single field of behaviour; of a landscape that is continuous between, beneath and through buildings that are themselves beautiful and adaptable, continuous through the horizontal and the vertical; of a spectacular centre, worthy of the rebirth of a great city at the heart of Europe.

The conversation continues, between Alsop and McLean, and between them and other friends: the project goes on.

BERLIN

STREET NAMES BASED ON SEASONS related to important dates in History.

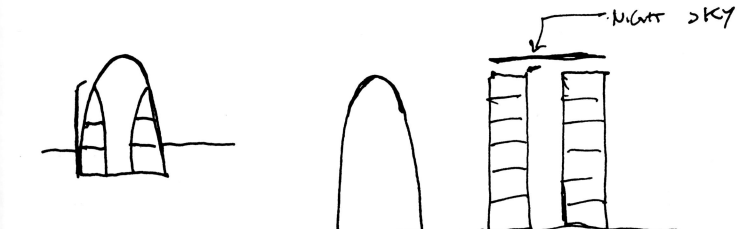

NIGHT SKY

Reflecting Glass SPRING STREET.

DIRECT VISUAL ACCESS FROM POINT TO POINT.

ABOVE

ARTIFICIAL SKY

BRIDGES

through trees

GROUND LINE

Below

BERLIN:

(PUBLIS) — light moderator
landscape

EARTH ......

Surface lights

service.

Create a landscape of elements that appear when
the climate is right.

PARALLEL
EXPERIENCES.

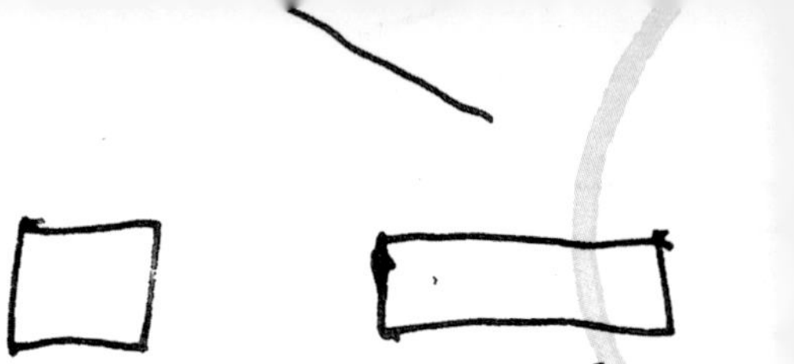

Berlin = A NAUGATY STREET.

Centre of points

2 phases — one of streets as

Stage ① object
+ points.

BETWEEN 2 stage — the spaces
The important parts in the day are usually
related to Meals. between.
No control — harzog fari

LINE OF NAMES
BOXES.

EGG.

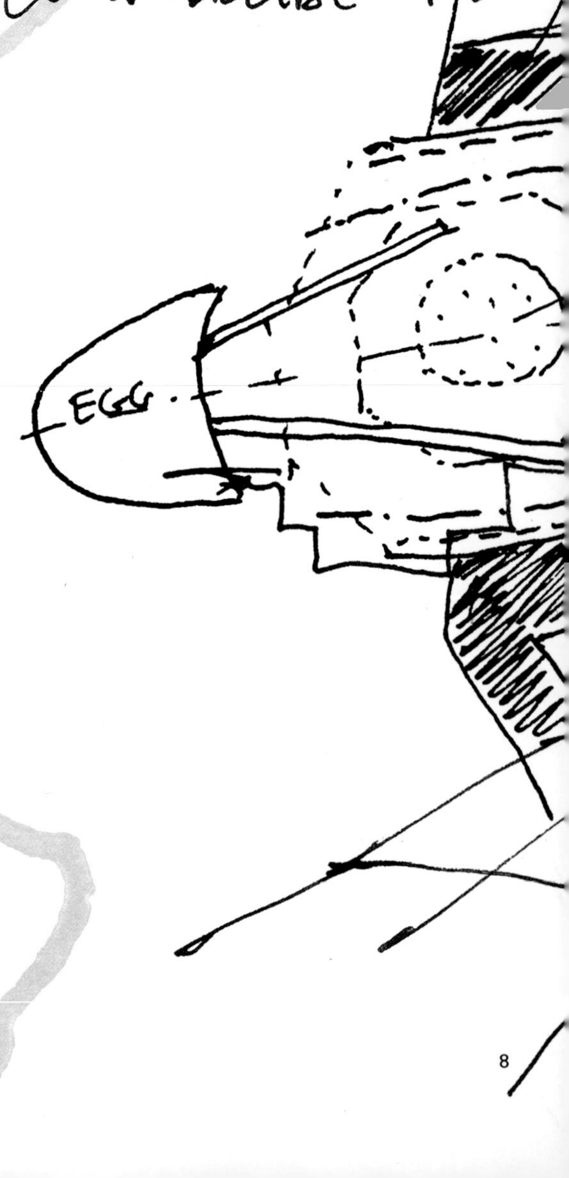

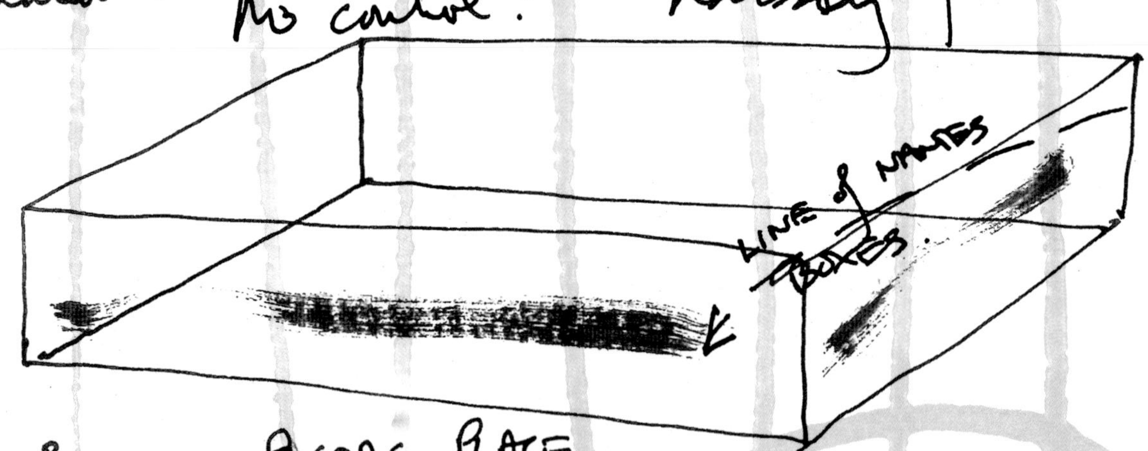

BERLIN PICNIC PLACE

Spaces

GRE
th

Commercial REAL

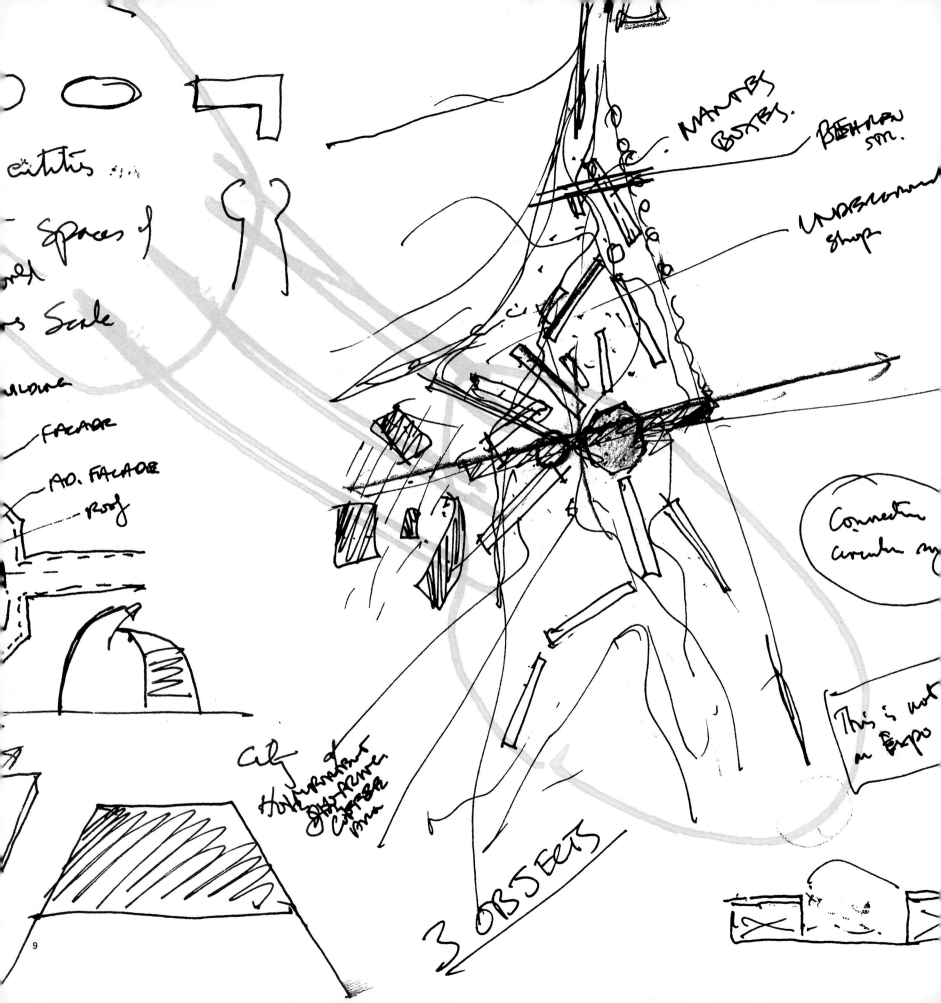

THE CENTRE AS AN
ART WORK
LIVING/PERFORMANCE

NO PLAN.

Demands of
the Future

For almost 45 years architecture had no place around the Berlin Wall. It was a swathe of city land physically denied to the imagination and to the ordinary exchanges of life. Except, of course, that the Wall itself lived in all our imaginations. And there were extraordinary human exchanges, some involving bullets. It was a barrier that, even though its actual life was historically brief, seemed eternal to at least two generations. It was one of the world's key monuments – a memory of one war and the promise of another. In symbolising the impossibility of rationally resolving one conflict, the Wall became a sub-architectural realisation of all human failure.

Yet suddenly it vanished. We were left with an odd and inscrutable vacuum. The conflict we had believed eternal turned out to be a temporary madness. Since 1945 the world had seemed so simple – a theatre of the Cold War in which communism and capitalism manœuvred and confronted. But the granite of communism turned to dust, its grand simplifications finally disproved. At the same time our simplification – symbolised by the Wall – was also disproved. The world was not just this one conflict, it was many.

So this city land was emptied of this one crude meaning. Ghosts still walked, of course. There were the ghosts of Kennedy and Kruschev as well as those of all who died trying to cross from East to West. There was the ghost of Hitler, a poisonous emanation from his bunker. And, beyond that, the millions of ghosts of a united Berlin, a real, undivided city as important, grand and exciting as any in the world.

Berlin was left with a space that was architecturally empty but replete with meaning and implication. At the most obvious level this space was an hiatus in the city plan. Streets and squares were severed and bisected. This gross intrusion into the organism of a city at once suggests an obvious solution: rebuild the streets, repair the squares, restore Berlin by applying an architectural Band-Aid or skin-graft to its wound.

But this was scarcely a time to succumb to the obvious. Here was an urban space like no other on the Earth. To any thoughtful architect it was an extraordinary challenge. First it was a vast space in what will probably be, once again, Europe's most important city. But, much more importantly, it was a space in which every gesture counted. Build modestly and you seem to deny the drama of the site and its past; build rhetorically or pompously and there are so many wrong things that could be said.

Of course, to a *really* thoughtful architect the answer, initially at least, is obvious: trust architecture and city life. A convincing solution to this site could not arise from developer's speculative trash, from infantile postmodernist games with the past, or from some pompous *grand projet*. All would feel, look and be self-consciously imposed, displaying imaginations crippled by the need to dominate and determine our sense of the past.

But architecture and city dwellers, left to their own devices, know how to cope with the past. They know it cannot be escaped or contained. Whatever you do, it will be there, if not physically on the site, then somewhere else. And certainly it will be inside your head. Nobody builds or lives in a pure unencumbered present. So there is no point in earnestly bowing to the past and trying to decipher its millions of messages. You are hearing them anyway. Get on with your shopping, get on with your work, get on with your architecture.

These are the terms in which Will Alsop and Bruce McLean see Berlin: as an *architectural* possibility. Their projection for the Potsdamer Platz and Leipziger Platz is both utterly specific to that site and yet utterly universal in its implications and ideas. It would be a scheme, above all, in which buildings regained their autonomy and importance as objects.

To understand this central point, it is necessary to disentangle some of the arcane debates that have taken place in architecture in this century. This process may not explain why the buildings are beautiful, but it may explain *how* they are.

The dominant movement of the age, modernism, suffered from an acute speech defect. What the modernists said was seldom what they meant and almost never what they did. The most laughable area of confusion was on the vexed issue of form and function. It was said – and still is – that modernism in one of its most influential incarnations was all about the rigorous realisation of function in form. Make your wall as ruthlessly wall-like as you could or your window as starkly window-like and beauty would inevitably follow.

The idea is infantile verging on the imbecilic. In some forms it was expressed with something of the naive fervour of Pol Pot announcing Year Zero in Cambodia. Its implication was that, somehow, architects were able to start again – to see windows and walls with the eyes of perfect innocence. Yet it was the expressed belief of many great modernists and the realised building practice of many third-raters.

One could list any number of similar examples of the way modernist doctrine undermined and almost discredited modernist achievement. As a result, a genius on the scale of Le Corbusier is often popularly seen as a cold, functional modernist – a bizarre and improbable insult to the designer of La Tourette or Ronchamp. Such idle, misguided history makes the work of the mediocre postmodernist easy. He simply has to glue on a few details to 'brighten the place up a bit' and he is assumed to be heroically rejecting the stern demands of a discredited style. Equally, mediocre late modernists could appear to be adhering faithfully to the style simply by reproducing the superficial 'feel' of modernism – its white walls, cool spaces and super-tasteful touches of colour.

The real effect of all this was to neutralise buildings. They were no longer available as objects of contemplation or celebration so much as design solutions. They were either good, tasteful, modernist design solutions or they were bright, splashy postmodernist design solutions. But they could not be buildings that defined places, celebrated the city, or simply looked a peculiar and interesting colour at sunset. In fact, they could not be buildings at all, only offices, shops or factories. The whole sculptural reality of architecture had been denied.

The history of Will Alsop's development takes in all this. His career began with the almost oppressive awareness that there was no particular reason why any particular building should be built in any particular style. This uncertainty was part of the inspiration of postmodernism and Alsop, when confronting the issue, began from a postmodernist position. But he swiftly realised the inherent exhaustion of the style – almost ten years, it should be said, before it dawned on everybody else.

His designs then began to work through a series of variations that seemed to be working their way between the lines of modernist orthodoxy. Certainly he would 'express' the function as the texts demanded, but in such a way that the relationship between expression and function gradually changed. The expression became a poetic commentary on the function and, sometimes, detached itself completely. Similarly, he would toy with modernist planning theories – like the division of functions – but in an almost maniacally thorough way so that his schemes became increasingly fragmented and 'disarticulate'.

The theme running through this process was the search for a way to escape from the enforced neutrality of modern architecture without simply resorting to incoherent and meaningless decoration. Alsop wanted assertive, sculptural buildings, but he saw the folly of a mindless rejection of modernist achievement. The aim was to let architecture be architecture in as full a sense as it was at La Tourette or the Parthenon. In such buildings form and function, decoration and structure are not slavishly locked in a single allowable equation; they are engaged in a fluid dance that never lets us walk away congratulating ourselves on having finally taken all that the building has to offer.

Alsop is a dynamic, unpredictable artist, so the next sentence may be unwise. Nevertheless, I think that, in his Berlin scheme, this process reaches a triumphant climax. A form of modernist planning is fully realised. There are summer and winter streets and rigorous divisions of functions. But, typically, this division has been taken far beyond the simple rationalism of 'good' design. His office towers are at the outer perimeter of the site so that arriving commuters will be obliged to pass through the intervening space. Bad modernism simple squeezed its functional layers together and produced the sealed-in life and drab spaces that characterise its most spectacular failures.

But the obligation on the commuter to be a real city dweller is hardly onerous. The freedom and variety of his experience in walking or roller-skating from train to office would be extended by a whole range of subtle changes of environment and perspective. He would not, in other words, be oppressed by the functionalism of his working day. It is not simply that there would be a lot to do, but also that there would be plenty to be.

And, of course, he could look at the towers themselves. There is something deliberately arbitrary about these structures. Clearly the actual office area required would determine their final form and size. But there is a deeper arbitrariness at work. They are beautiful shapes, not because of anything that goes on inside, but because, well, they are beautiful shapes.

Colour, however, is the real symbol of their liberation. Alsop's use of colour has, over the years, been moving slowly towards this aggressive freedom. In the Berlin collaboration with McLean that progress has arrived at a remarkable new extreme. Modernism had, in its later incarnations, drifted towards tasteful grays and blues. Certainly bright splashes of other colours occurred, but they were not free, In Richard Rogers' Pompidou Centre, for example, the service ducts are lavishly painted, but they could only be justified as coding for the different types of function. It was as if the ethical purism of modernism could not quite be shaken off.

But, Alsop realised, this puritan fear of colour was yet another way in which buildings were being neutralised. They were not allowed to be coloured unless the colour was either obviously tasteful or inward-looking in that it referred directly to function. Why bother? There was nothing to be afraid of. Alsop's colour for his Berlin scheme signals yet again that architecture can regain its autonomy as beautiful building.

Many architects – indeed, many members of the public – may feel a certain vertigo on contemplating this type of freedom. Surely there is some reason why this cannot be done, why it must not be allowed. But there is not. We are permitted to be architects.

And this brings us back to this site with exquisite symmetry. For what if we had thought about knocking down the Berlin Wall a few years ago? Surely there was some reason why this could not be done, why it must not be allowed. Remove the wall and we would suffer vertigo, standing at the edge of an alien abyss. But the Wall just vanished and we have not fallen. We are permitted to be free.

Bryan Appleyard

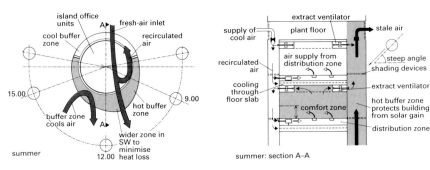

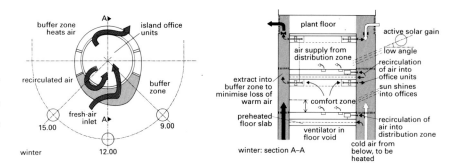

summer

tower

summer: section A–A

winter

winter: section A–A

Buildings as
Reptiles

The competition site offered special environmental challenges. It was necessary to recreate the bustling commercial centre that Potsdamer Platz used to be and – equally important – to create spaces of high environmental quality both for the workers in the buildings and for those passing through the area.

Buildings consume almost 50 per cent of prime energy in Germany and are responsible for approximately 50 per cent of the country's carbon-dioxide production. They are also large consumers of CFCs and other noxious gasses.

City centres rely on air conditioning to satisfy their workers but this kind of solution is no longer tenable and other answers must be found. The implementation of environmentally responsive structures can significantly reduce energy consumption and, therefore, carbon-dioxide production while offering space of equal or better quality than air-conditioned buildings. Passive design is the intelligent use of natural resources.

There were three levels of concern:

Global (Macro)
– to reduce carbon-dioxide emissions, use of harmful materials and
   non-renewable woods
– to limit energy use

Local (Micro)
– to create sunlit, sheltered spaces
– to provide green space
– to use fresh, clean air from the gardens
– to provide an improved ecosystem for wildlife
– to limit traffic disruption and noise pollution

Internal (Office Environment)
– to create daylit buildings
– to use natural environmental conditioning where feasible
– to maintain good indoor air quality
– to give occupants personal control over their environment

In simple terms, the approach is based on the necessity of creating a comfortable and safe matrix of internal and external spaces for people to occupy. The assumption is that this will be achieved passively, rather than with systems. This means that the building fabric itself, its shape, form, planning and structure, must moderate the adverse effects of climate and yet take advantage of free natural energy – sun, wind, rain, geothermal resources.

Thus, like a cold-blooded reptile which raises its scales to warm itself in the sun and finds a shady rock when it needs to cool down, so our buildings need to be responsive and intelligent rather than inactive and dumb.

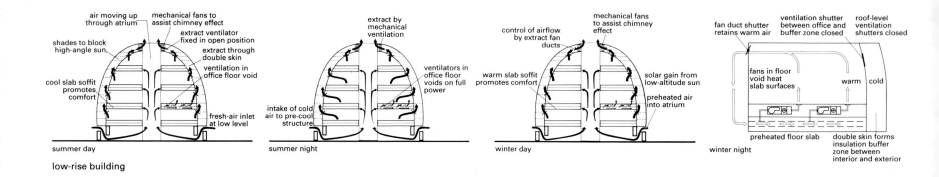

air moving up through atrium
mechanical fans to assist chimney effect
shades to block high-angle sun
extract ventilator fixed in open position
extract through double skin
ventilation in office floor void
cool slab soffit promotes comfort
fresh-air inlet at low level

summer day

low-rise building

extract by mechanical ventilation
ventilators in office floor voids on full power
intake of cold air to pre-cool structure

summer night

mechanical fans to assist chimney effect
control of airflow by extract fan ducts
warm slab soffit promotes comfort
solar gain from low-altitude sun
preheated air into atrium

winter day

fan duct shutter retains warm air
ventilation shutter between office and buffer zone closed
roof-level ventilation shutters closed
fans in floor void heat slab surfaces
warm   cold
preheated floor slab
double skin forms insulation buffer zone between interior and exterior

winter night

The design team aimed to achieve the following:

– to maximise human comfort in terms of thermal control, air quality, daylight, humidity, acoustics, and security
– to minimise running costs by making the maximum use of free energies – sun, wind, ground water, and daily temperature variation
– to maximise usable space by minimising both the plant area and the air-distribution-space requirement, by maximising structure/service integration, removing the necessity for false ceilings, and by structural efficiency
– to minimise capital cost by reducing the size of mechanical services, reducing the complexity of services, and, again, by structural efficiency

Workers are today applying pressure on managements in order to get better lighting and acoustics, fresh air, and greater personal temperature control. Environmental quality can transform an ordinary work space into one that actively enhances the productivity of the workforce without necessarily any extra cost to the client. The Alsop development sets out to achieve comfort by passive means – where possible this involves natural ventilation and the careful use of buffer zones.

These buffer zones play an important part in the architecture of the environmental systems. They inform and generate an architectural response rather than restrict Alsop's ideas. They are used to moderate and control heat loss and gain, to distribute excess heat to areas of a building which need it, and to distribute free cooling where it is required.

The height of the tallest buildings in the development means that opening windows are only possible at the lower levels – the wind pressures generated are too high to maintain any natural ventilation control. It is necessary to have a sealed skin, and this takes on its own human-like response: according to the season it can distribute heat or coolness around its perimeter.

The low-rise blocks use a different system. Where the surroundings permit opening windows, the buildings rely on cross-ventilation via an atrium heat-stack effect. Exposed concrete ceilings play an important part in maintaining thermal stability. In summer they are cooled with night air and absorb heat during the day. In winter they act as a thermal flywheel, preventing the buildings from cooling too quickly. In areas where pollution or noise are too great, an external buffer-zone skin can be used to draw air through a central atrium, up and through the skin. Again, exposed structural thermal mass is used to make air conditioning unnecessary.

Guy Battle
Ove Arup & Partners

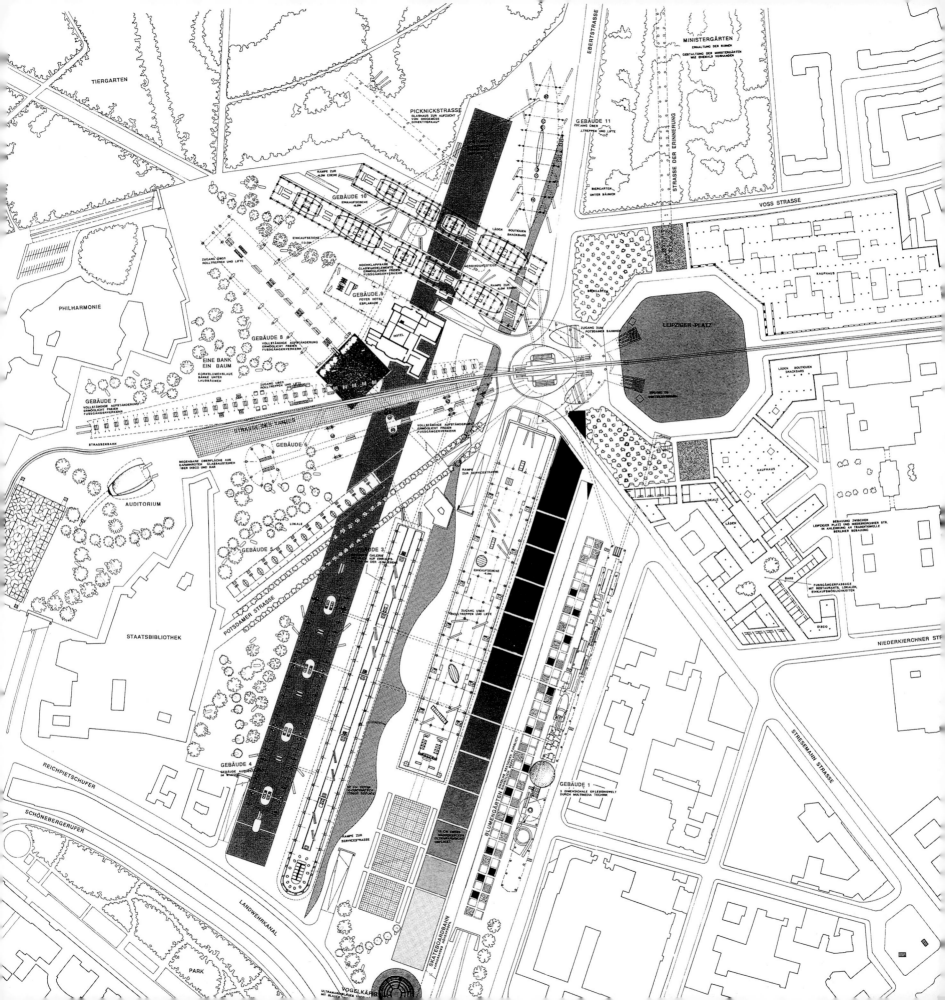

Potsdamer Platz/Leipziger Platz:
real places inscribed with irony.
Laid waste:
waiting for new beginnings.
Waiting
to be impelled towards wakefulness.

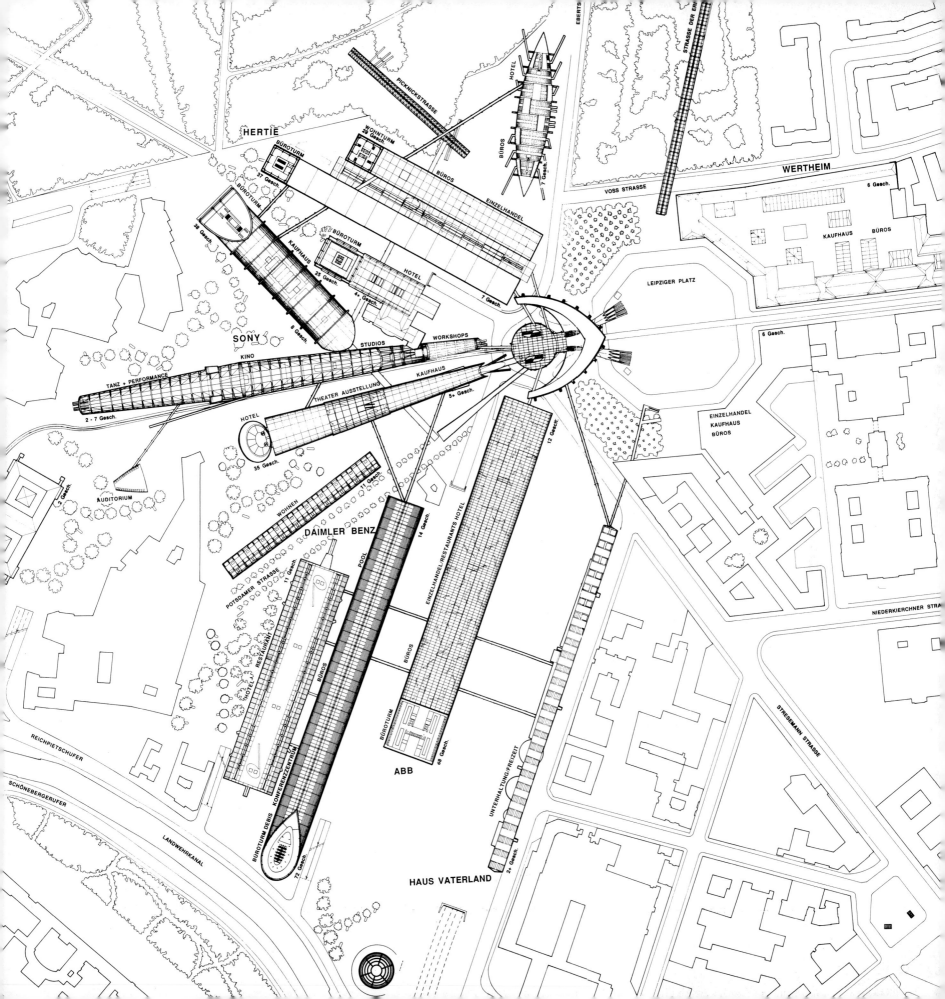

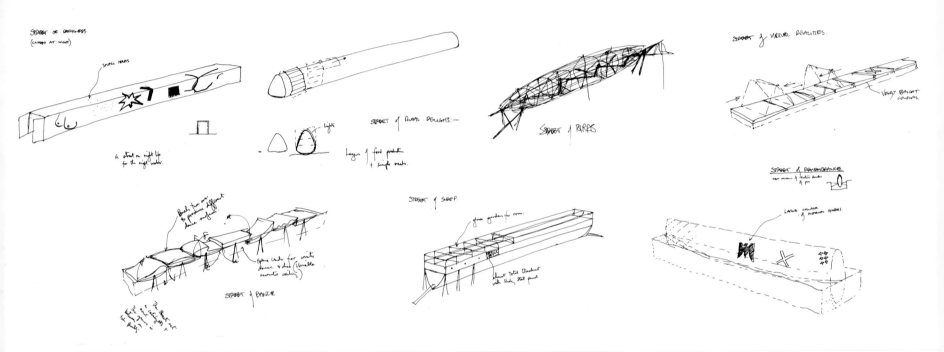

STREET OF DARKNESS
(CLOSED AT NIGHT)

SMALL FIRES

a street on night life
for the night worker.

lights

STREET OF RURAL DELIGHTS:-

began of food production
+ simple meals.

STREET OF FIRES.

STREET OF VIRTUAL REALITIES.

VERY BRIGHT
COLOURS

STREET OF REMEMBRANCE

LARGE COLUMN
OF MEMORIAL SPHERES.

STREET OF DANCE

STREET OF SLEEP.

grass garden for room.

STREET OF PHYSICAL ABUSE ? 51-3364 (MR CLAPPERTON)

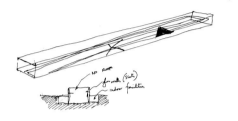

THE GROUND BELONGS TO THE PEOPLE — (TAKE AIR TO THE INTERIORS)

Berlin

Notes

1 It is a project of three levels:

Level −1
servicing and parking

Ground level
tablecloth of air and summer

Level +1
streets of shopping and leisure.

2 The proposal is **contextual** in the sense that it takes the city of objects (Kulturforum) and extends the idea of the randomly placed building into the idea of randomly placed streets (as objects). The west side of Leipziger Platz is built at the traditional Berlin height of 22 metres. Half-way across Leipziger Platz the city centre becomes a city of spaces (streets) – not objects.

3 The City of Objects allows a deliberate ambiguity between **urban space** and open **park space**. This ambiguity can be enjoyed in different ways in different seasons.

In winter the buildings are the streets, offering protection from the east wind and providing a level of comfort that will allow the new centre to be enjoyed.

In summer the parkland is used as the streets, allowing air to be freely circulated between the Canal and the Tiergarten. These spaces can also be used to provide areas for performances and exhibitions. They literally become an **indeterminate theatre**.

The surface of the park varies, to support different activities; i.e. the 100mm-deep water areas allow for ice events in winter.

In spring and autumn the whole area of interiors and exteriors is unified into a whole.

4 In order to achieve the relationships between inside and outside as described above, the buildings have to be designed in a particular way. They must be energy-efficient and variable. They must be capable of responding to climatic variation and different uses by being able to open up in different ways. This allows air and people to be circulated in a variety of ways. **Alternative theories are inappropriate to this environment.**

5 The place is also about saturated colour. Colour which will change with light is dynamic. We intend to use colour in a very powerful way.

6 This scheme is also about the night. It will appear to vary in form and transparency between day and night – a 24-hour place (if German shopping hours are allowed to change).

7 **Our streets are horizontal and vertical.**

8 The Mercedes Building is clad in leather, veneer and chromium.

9 **Buildings** have towers at one end of the streets to promote movement although still.

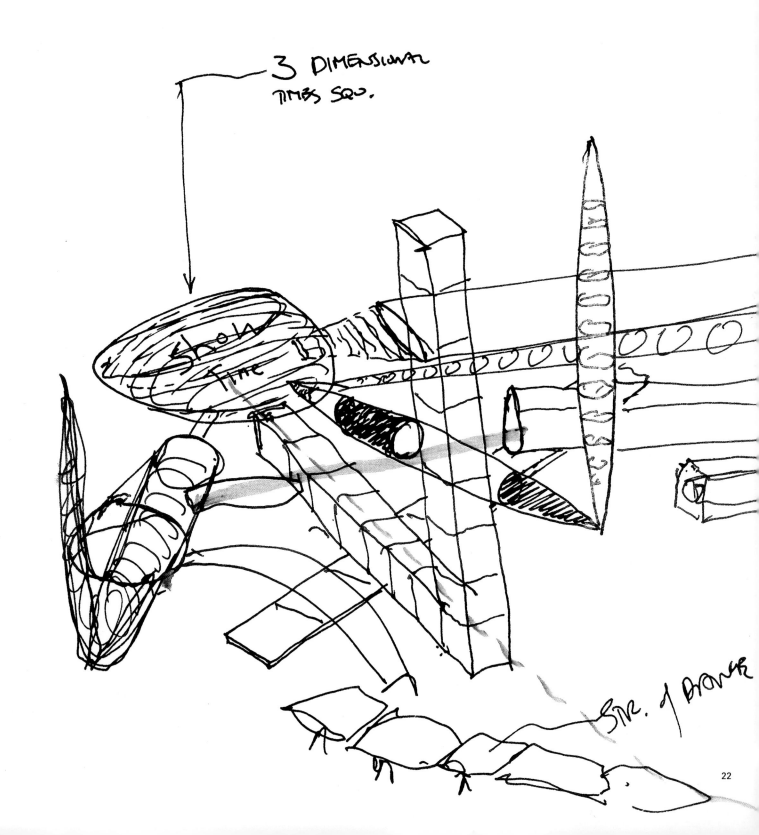

3 DIMENSIONAL
TIMES SQ.

STR. 1 BRONZE

22

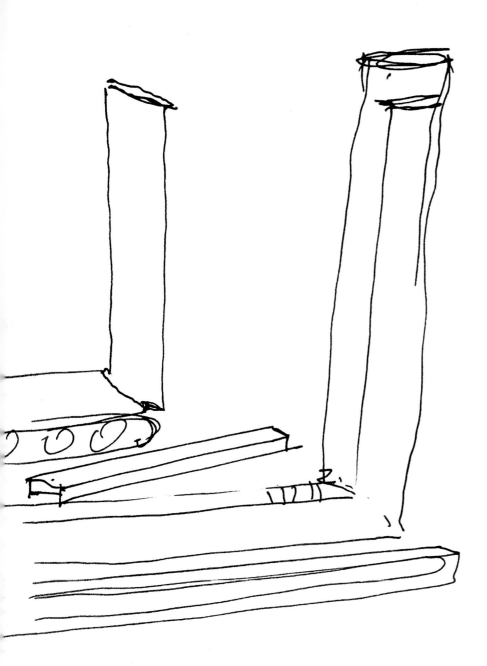

'Sometimes it becomes necessary to make a statement. Irony may be necessary to a statement: a means to complexify; a means towards getting closer to the truth. A statement is not a comment, it is an act.'
(McLean 1986)

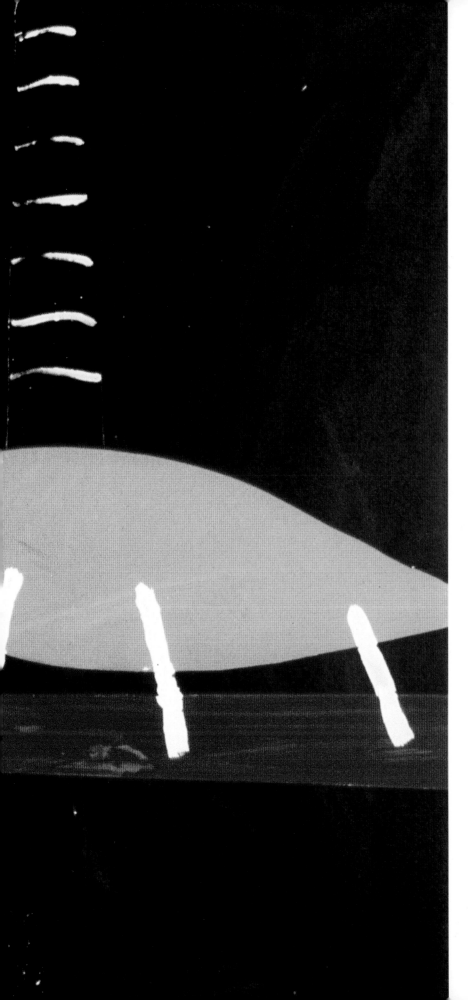

a polychrome
city centre The end of white modernism: the beginnings of

a new modernism (*among others*)

Antecedents: Le Corbusier's vision/Kiesler's bio-technics/Plečnik's urbane convivialities: the spirit not the letter.

considerations: Release of energy

Joy (see Blake: Energy is Eternal Delight.) Cf. Le Corbusier on the 'psychology of the art of building': 'sensibility, psycho-physiological reaction, security, the treasure of collected things. At the same time, the flood of inventions, the joy of discovery, splendour and pangs of creation. Participation in action; to be in harmony with the signs of our time, to take part, to live, *the notion of well-being*' (my italics)

'Through architecture I wish to help people live better. I want to bring a sense of dignity, of joy ... Joy, what a fantastic word! No need to shut everything in!' (Alsop 1991)

Love of the natural world: responsibility to it

Making space for play

Denial of historicism

Extensions of technology determined by behavioural possibilities, not limited by functional givens

new forms
new things to do

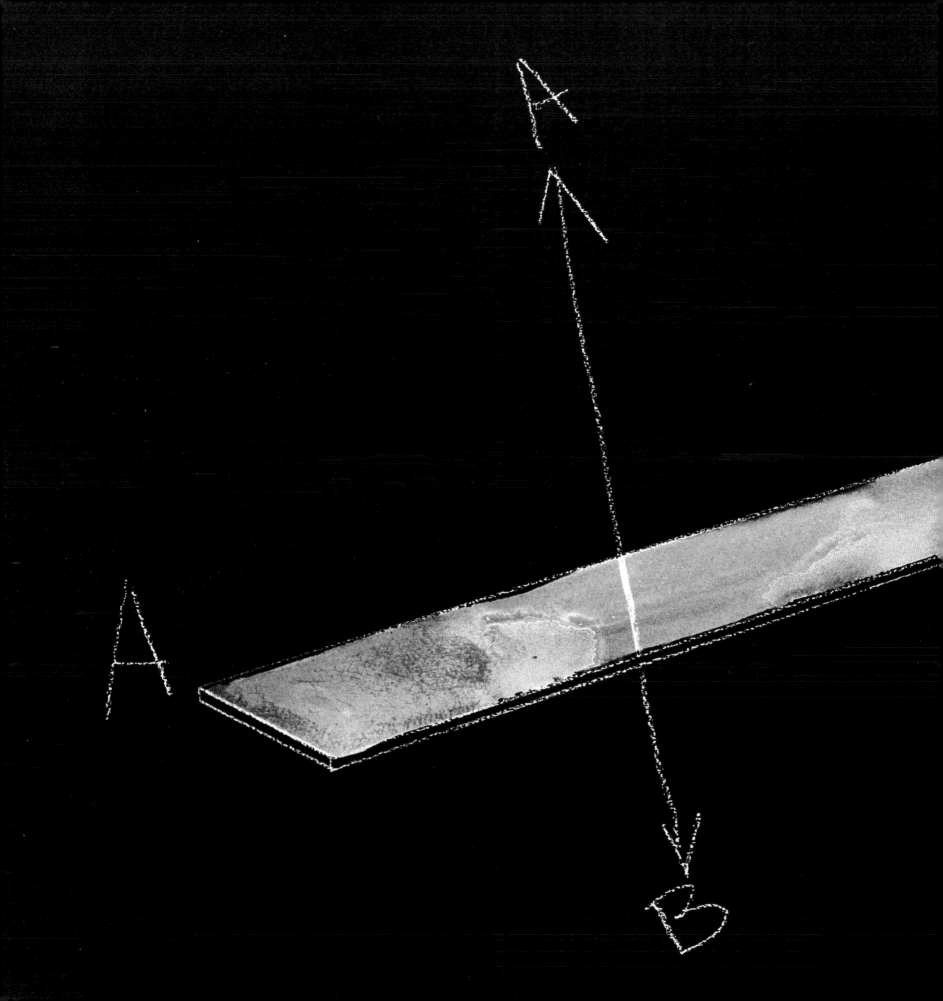

THIS STREET IS NOT A CANYON.

The drawings dividing the sections of this book have all been made since the competition result was known. The opportunity has been taken to re-examine the concept of the 'street'.

It is particularly pertinent because the competition-winning entry by Heinz Hilmer and Christopher Sattler is composed of streets and places that totally reject, without question, any way of living in a city other than arranging buildings around pieces of the Earth's surface which happen to be long and narrow. There is no sense of enquiry for Berlin in the winning project. Berlin will remain an idea about the nineteenth century.

People behave in new ways.

My starting point is that buildings in cities prevent you travelling from A to B along the shortest route. For this reason, the whole area covered by the competition was considered to be a street. A street with no buildings. What could such a street be?

It could be considered as a large table which could be laid in different ways for different occasions.

A field of behaviour

Italo Calvino writing 16 years before the Wall crumbled:

'When Marx was writing, and for some time afterward, the "Do Not Enter" sign on the road to utopian projects meant one should concentrate all one's thought and practice on criticising, and formulating a strategy of attack against, the only society actually in existence, and this implied an austere and demanding discipline. But as soon as an alternative society came into being, and the experimental fluidity and effervescence of its beginning (which could indeed be called utopian) was followed by an official apologetics for the present as if the present were the most desirable of all futures, then a veto took effect – explicitly or implicitly – on efforts to imagine any model but the existing one.'

(*plus ça change … plus ça change …*)

WORLDS
BIGGEST
ANNING

32

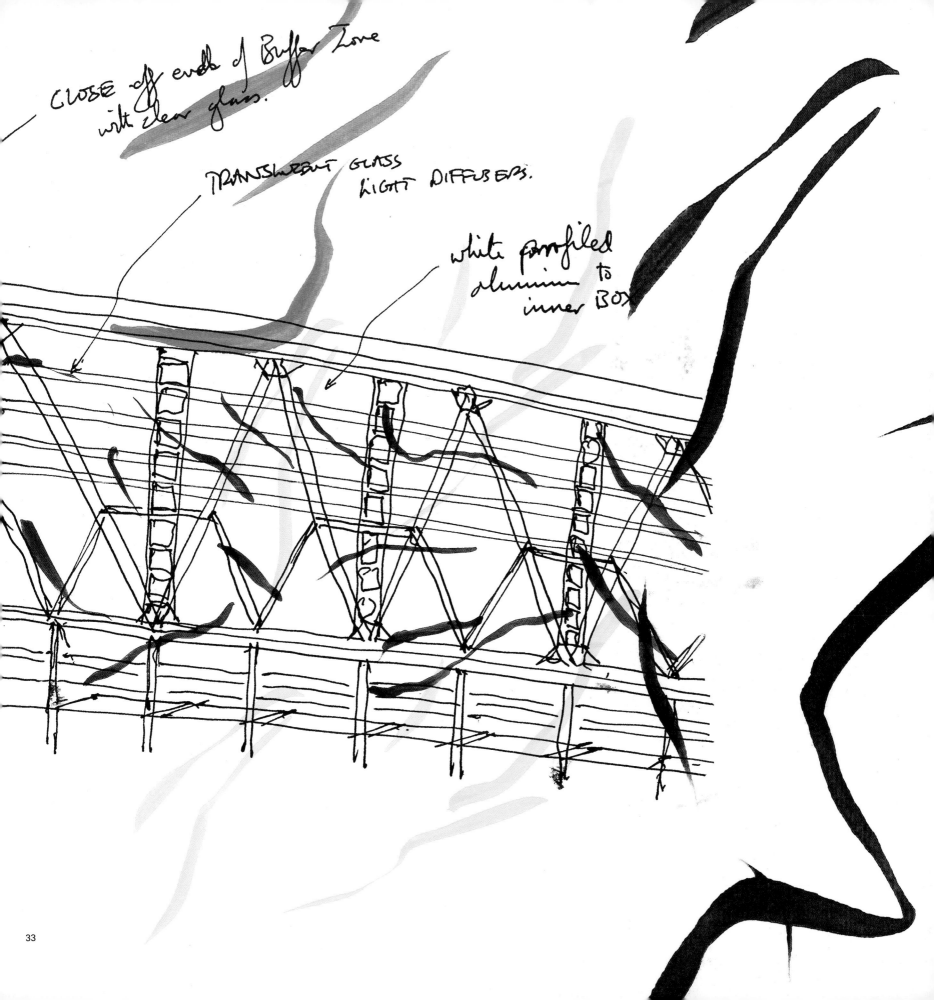

CLOSE off ends of Buffer Zone
with clear glass.

TRANSLUCENT GLASS
LIGHT DIFFUSERS.

white profiled
aluminium to
inner BOX

33

ABB Building

Internal 'boxes' are clad in white profiled aluminium with strip windows into the office spaces. Solar shading is provided by horizontally projecting etched glass blinds spanning between the internal boxes and the external glass skin. The space between the inner and outer skins forms an environmental control buffer zone and, along the centre, a wide atrium. The external glazing is coloured and patterned.

Sketches for the ABB Building show the tail end extended with the world's biggest awning.

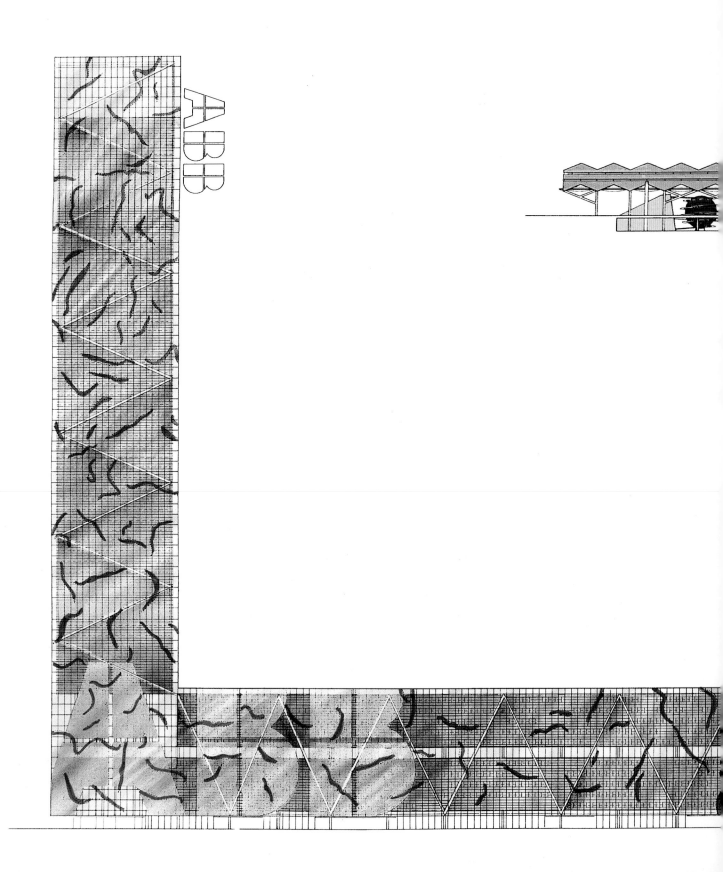

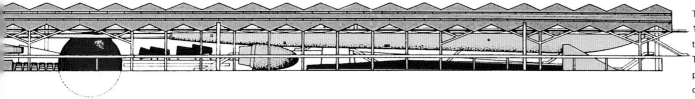

Hausvaterland

The 'theme' restaurant of the 1930s is reinstated on the original site, and updated. The experimental pleasure park lies half in and half out of the ground. Every kind of 'virtual' experience is provided – giant magic motion machines, an enormous 'living' model of the Earth, 360° cinema, artificial gravity, sensory deprivation, and a machine for giving Berliners a sense of their own presence relative to the cosmos.

Supported on three columns above the park is a terrace of traditionally planned two-bedroom flats.

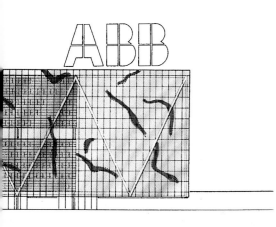

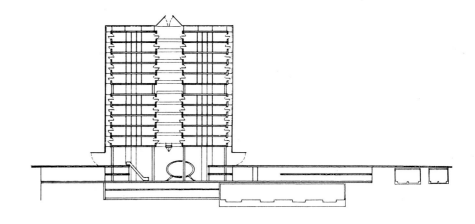

IS

A SURFACE

Potsdamer Platz/Leipziger Platz: central
Berlin 1991/92:

'The tradition of all the dead generations
weighs like a nightmare on the brain of
the living' (Marx)

a polychrome
city centre: open/radial/useful/indeterminate:
a new beginning (cf. Beuys: 'new beginnings
are in the offing!')

a way of waking from the nightmare of history

A new modernism is demanded: without
the certainties of the old modernisms,
but with a comparable vision and hope.
Realistic.

[cf. 'the poetic spirit' that imbues the
utopian systematising of Fourier:
'...Marx and Engels point out the
contrast between the "systematic form"
and the "real content" of the system,
which remains the ultimate way of
reading him (and not only him), a way
that has now been developed and
redefined very accurately by Roland
Barthes as the contrast between *system*
and *systematic*.' – Calvino]

Realistic (provisional) = hopeful (not
optimistic)

Truth is realism

(the real is complex/dialectical/
ambiguous/paradoxical/unpredictable/
verifiable/mysterious/surprising)

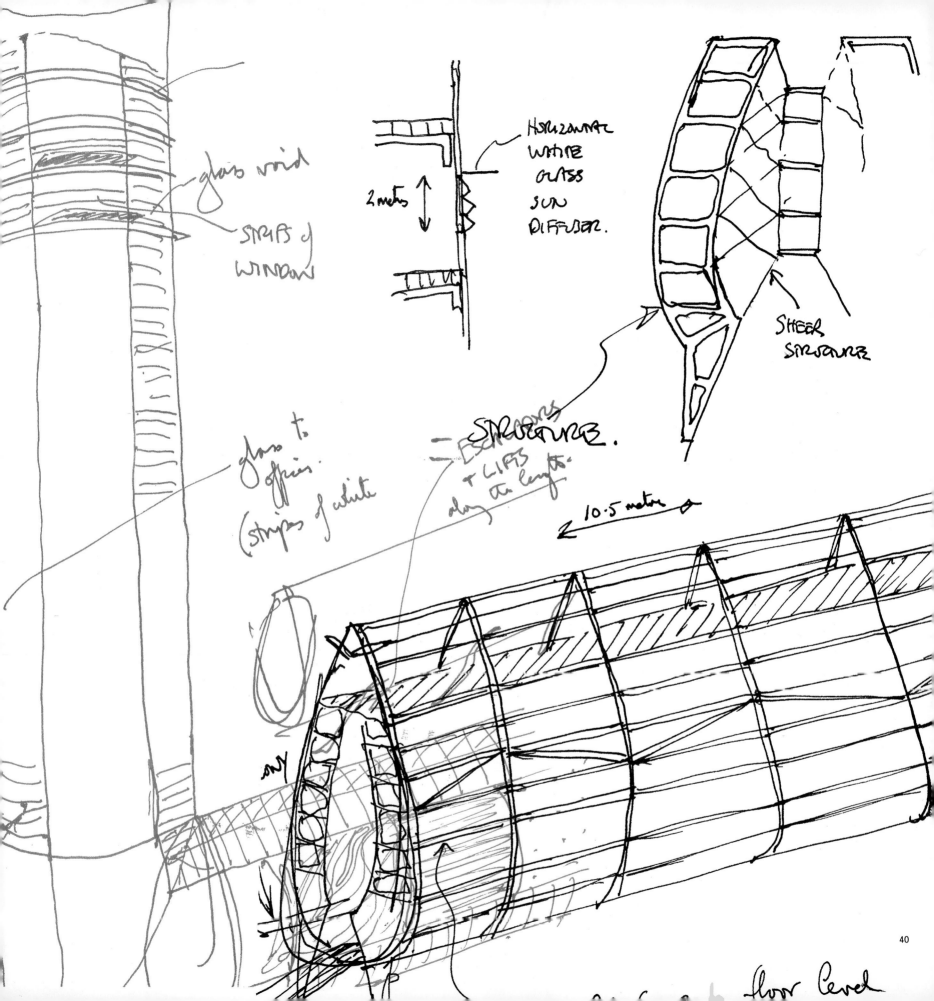

glass void

STRIPS of WINDOW

glass to offices. (stripes of white

HORIZONTAL WHITE GLASS SUN DIFFUSER.

2 metres

SHEER STRUCTURE

STRUCTURE.

ESCALATORS + LIFTS along the length.

10.5 metres

any

floor level

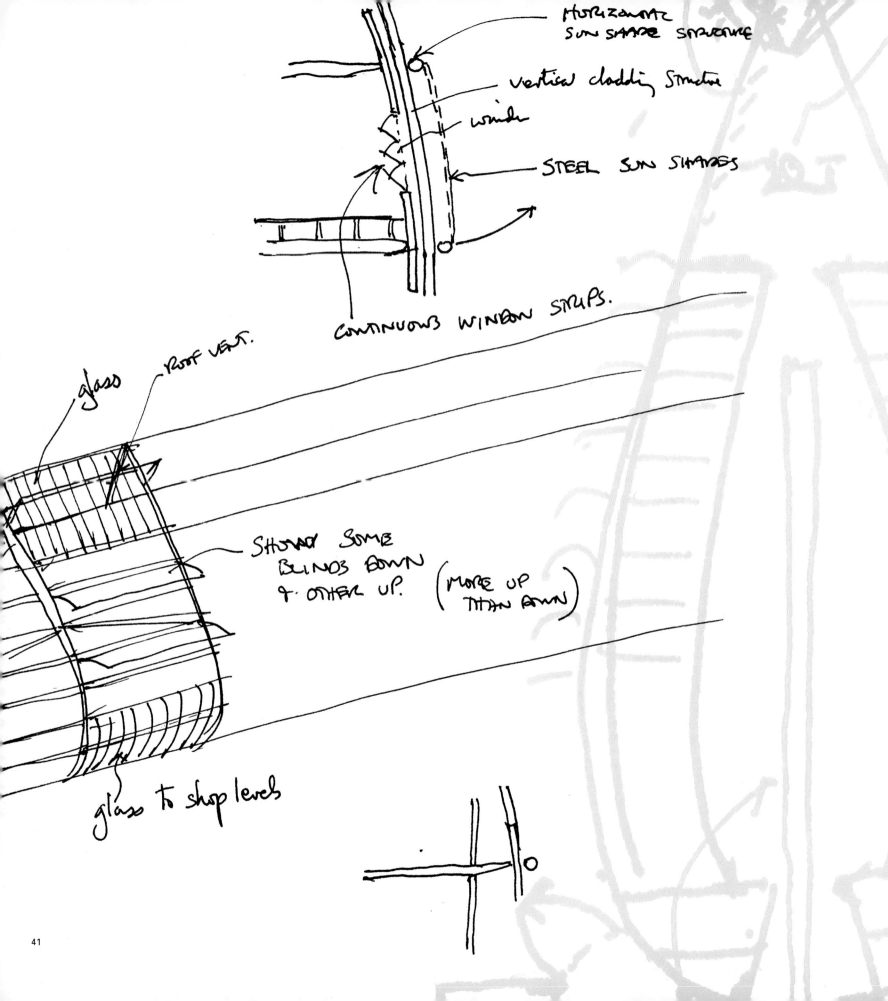

HORIZONTAL
SUN SHADE STRUCTURE

VERTICAL CLADDING STRUCTURE

WINDOW

STEEL SUN SHADES

CONTINUOUS WINDOW STRIPS.

ROOF VENT.

glass

SHOULD SOME
BLINDS DOWN
& OTHER UP. (MORE UP
THAN DOWN)

glass to shop levels

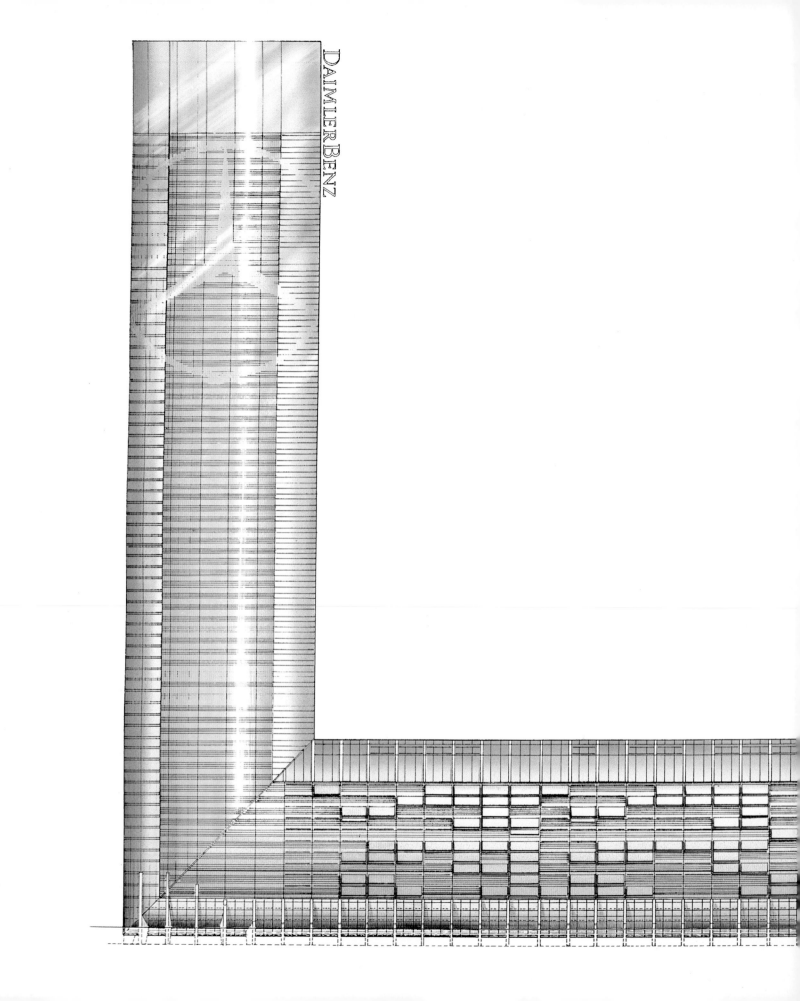

Daimler Benz Building

As with several of the other tower structures, the floorplate form of the DB tower is identical to the cross-section of the horizontal street element of the building. The back and front edges of the tower have clear glazing – the floor slabs inside stop short of the external wall, creating spectacular naturally lit vertical circulation voids.

The top 30 metres of the tower is a clear glazed box, without internal features. Shops occupy the lower three storeys and a subterranean undercroft. The finishes of the tower are, of course, intended to reflect the opulence and style of Mercedes cars.

The structure of the tower is a rigid shell – the outer walls provide the stiffness. This is the best means of achieving minimum width relative to height. Seen from the front (the south), the tower appears to be very slender for its height. At the lower level, the shell structure is supported by a ring of massive inclined concrete legs like those that support the steel structure.

A swimming pool runs the length of the horizontal leg of the building, occupying a space in the glass ridge. The pool is 41 metres wide and 400 metres long.

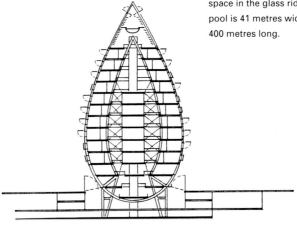

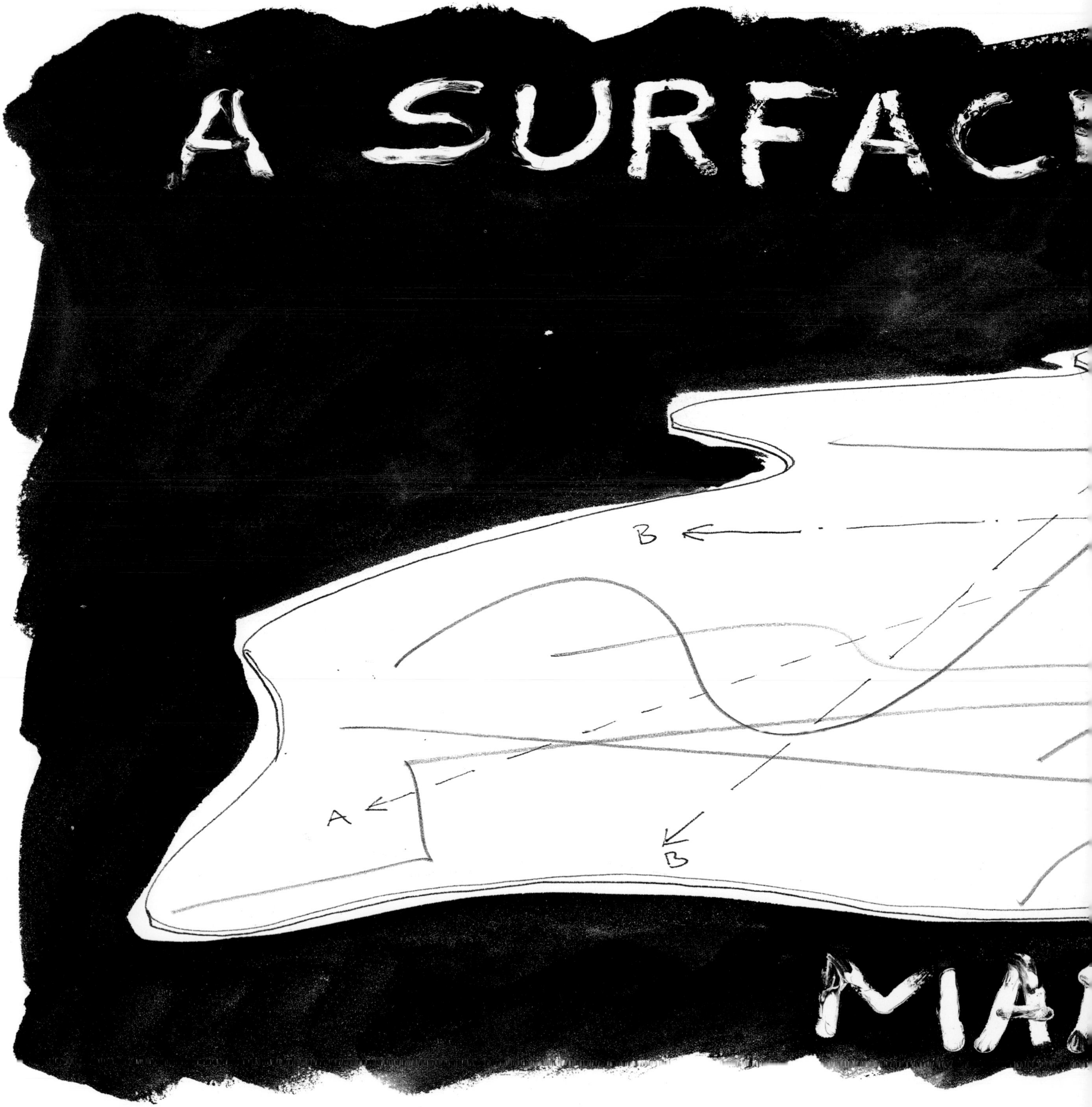
A SURFAC
B
A
B
MIA

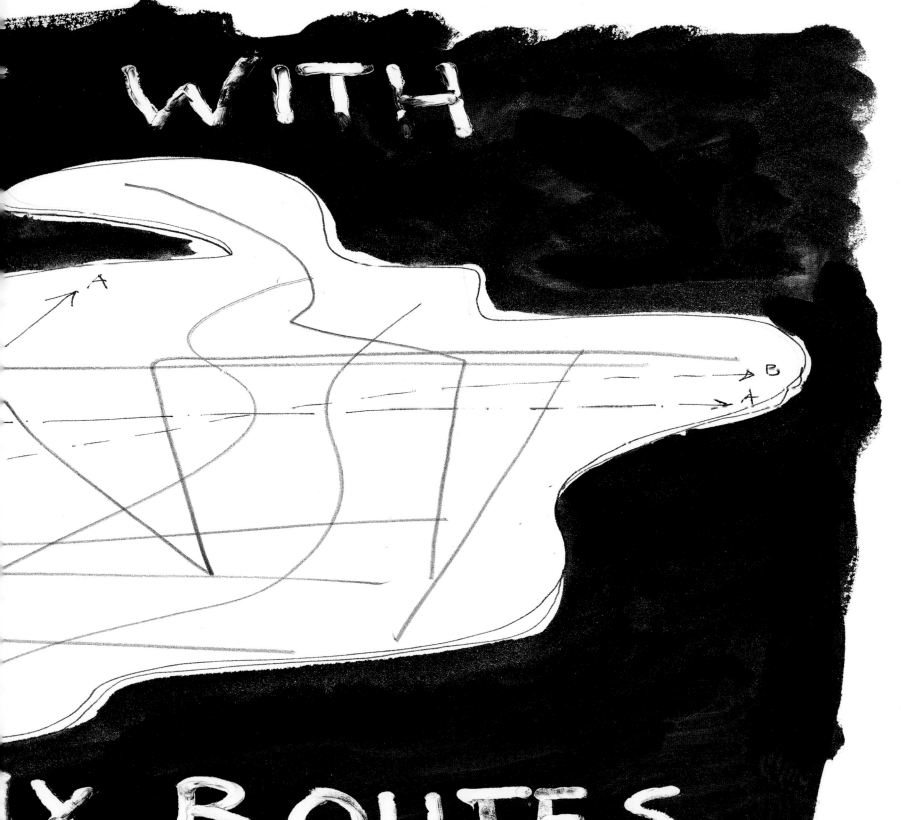

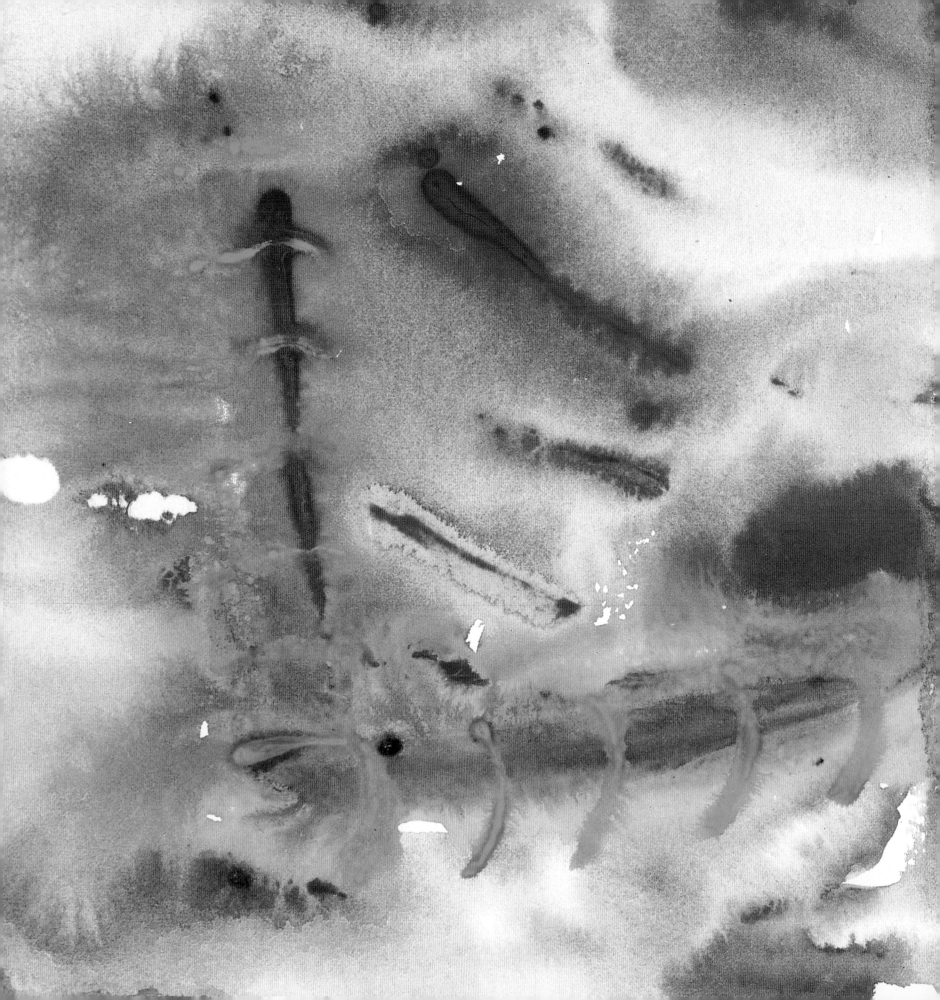

Mercedes Strasse
u TURM
A place to work
contemplate &
shop to death

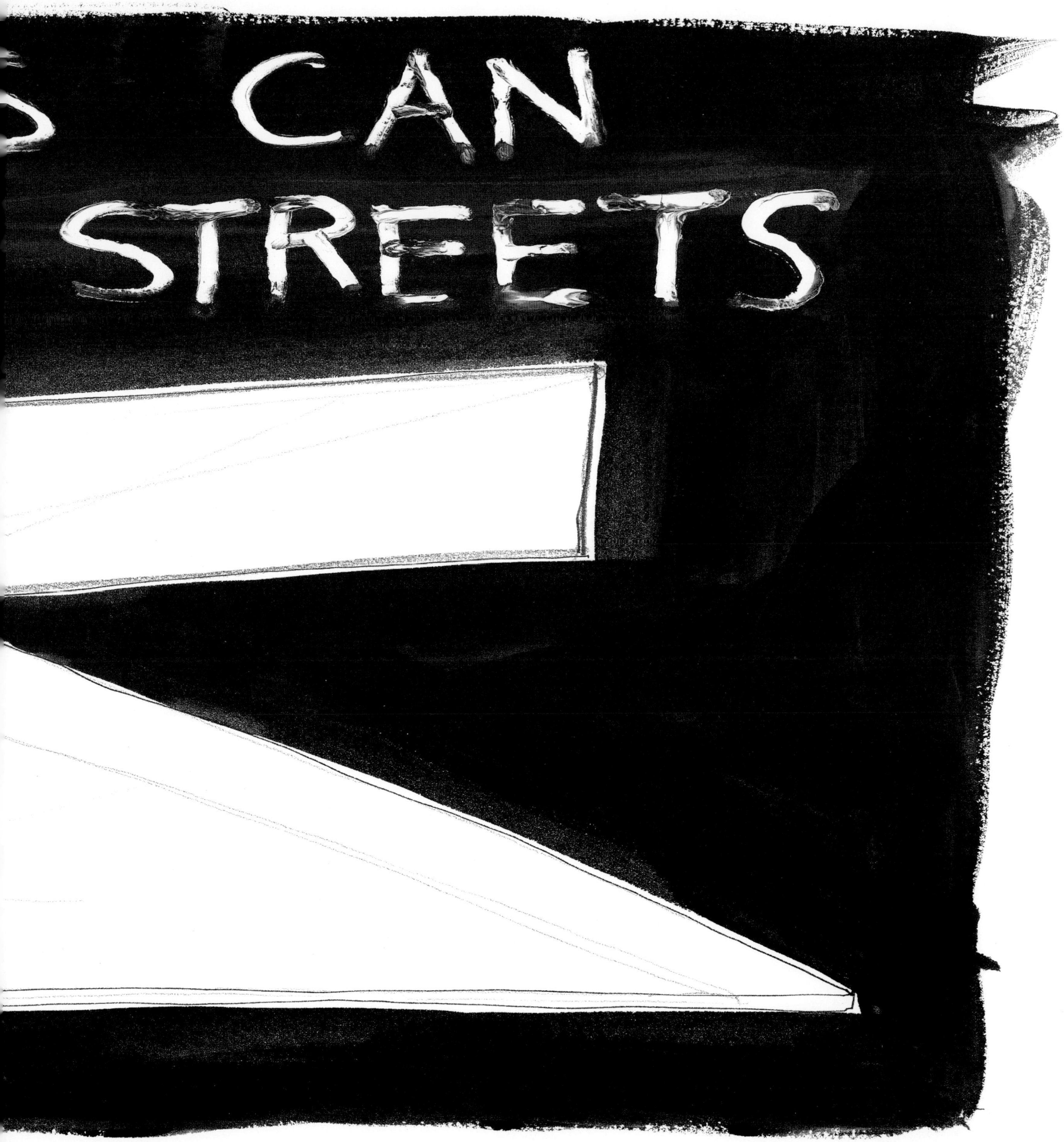
CAN
STREETS

the
idea: a landscape independent of the buildings;
around them, beneath them; through
them. A landscape at once topographical
and phenomenological: we move through
it; it moves through us. *As a fact* we
carry it from open air into the sheltered
streets that radiate from the focal point.

The landscape as a function of weather:
not merely looked at, but felt, something
to be avoided at inclement times.
[Architecture = 'shelter (of people, of
things, of work, of institutions, of ideas)' –
Le Corbusier]

A landscape traversed without
impediment (cf. Cedric Price: 'The main
problem with cities is that the buildings
get in the way of walking from a to b').

A *landscape* capable of transformation;
not a fixed *park*, encoded forever.

A plain/a plane. An empty page/not a
grand *platz*, encoded.

'It must change'

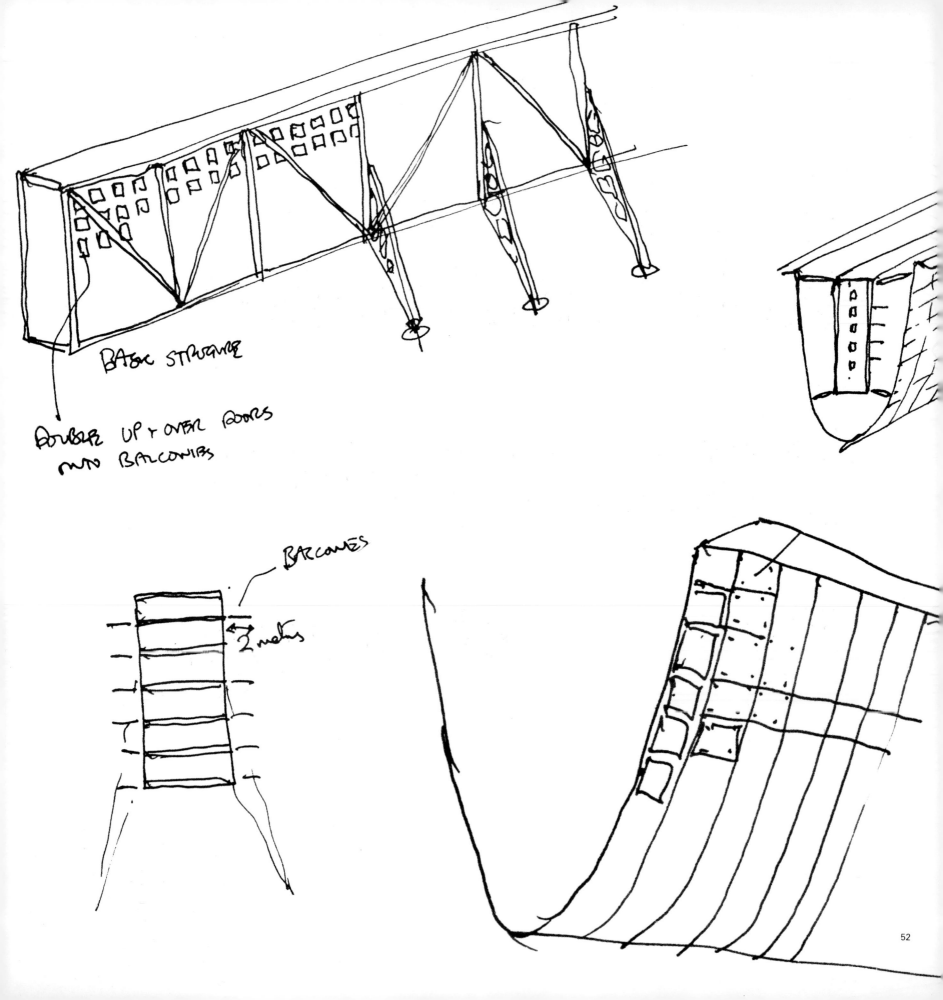

BASIC STRUCTURE

DOUBLE UP + OVER DOORS
INTO BALCONIES

BALCONIES

2 metres

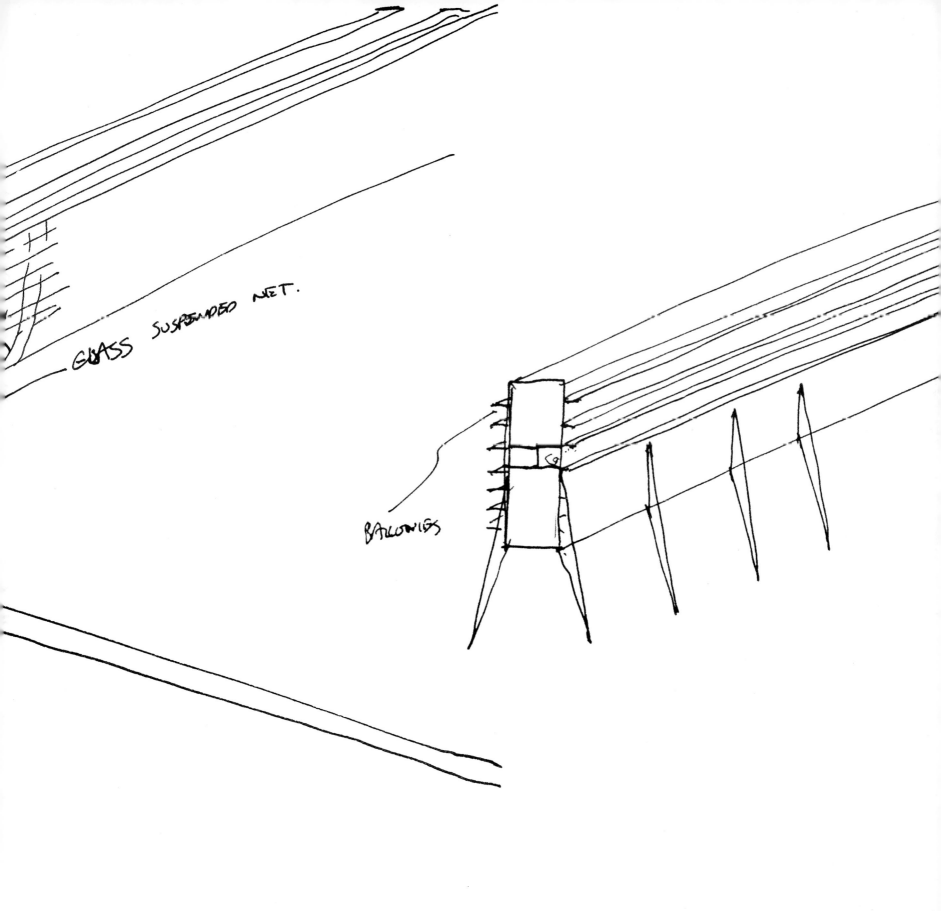

GLASS SUSPENDED NET.

BALCONIES

Daimler Benz Hotel

The form of this building is a development of the climatic buffer-zone idea. The hotel accommodation is contained within a simple concrete-framed slab. This has square punched openings in its sides, each of which is a floor-to-ceiling 'door' into a hotel room. The openings are covered by glazed 'upslover' doors. When opened, the doors give access to 2-metre wide balconies – wide enough to be used a habitable spaces. The balconies cantilever into the semi-external void of a huge buffer zone.

The external skin of the building is a hanging chain structure, suspended from the top edge of the inner block by cantilever arms and looping all the way round, beneath the inner block. The inner block is raised on 15-metre-high legs to allow the glass parabola to curve around beneath.

The environment in the balcony zone would always be a moderated version of the external environment – cool and balmy on hot summer days, warm and cosy on freezing winter days.

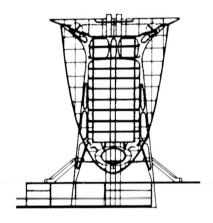

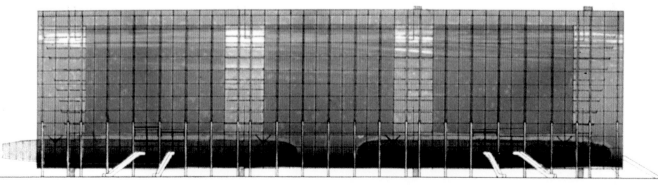

Daimler Benz Housing
200 flats

The north-western side has a free-standing, full-height glazed screen. The floors of the flats can be rolled out to bridge the gap between the building and the glass wall. The solid fascias of the main block are clad in different materials – one material for each floor – without any repetition. Metals, woods, coloured glass and cementitious panelling are all used.

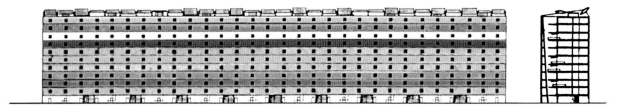

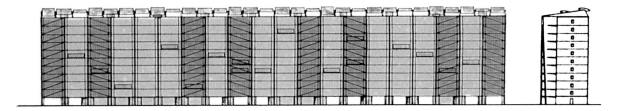

THE BUILDING CAN BE

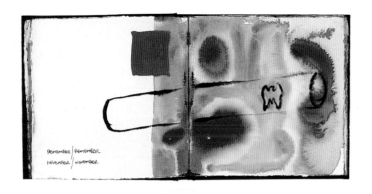

REMEMBER / REMEMBER
NOVEMBER / NOVEMBER

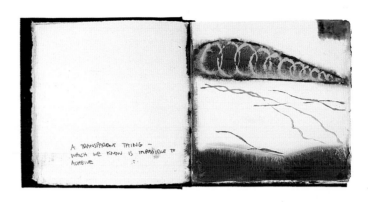

A TRANSPARENT THING —
WHICH WE KNOW IS IMPOSSIBLE TO
ACHEIVE

PEOPLE IN THE VERTICAL
BIRDS IN THE HORIZONTAL.

A DOUBLE TAPERED HANCOCK TOWER
(A POSSIBILITY — BUT DOUBTFUL)

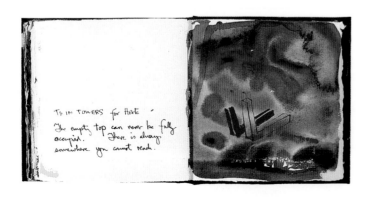

TWIN TOWERS FOR HERE —
The empty top can never be fully
occupied. There is always
somewhere you cannot reach.

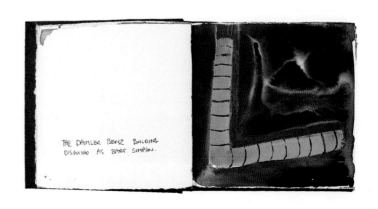

THE DAIMLER BENZ BUILDING
DISGUISED AS BART SIMPSON.

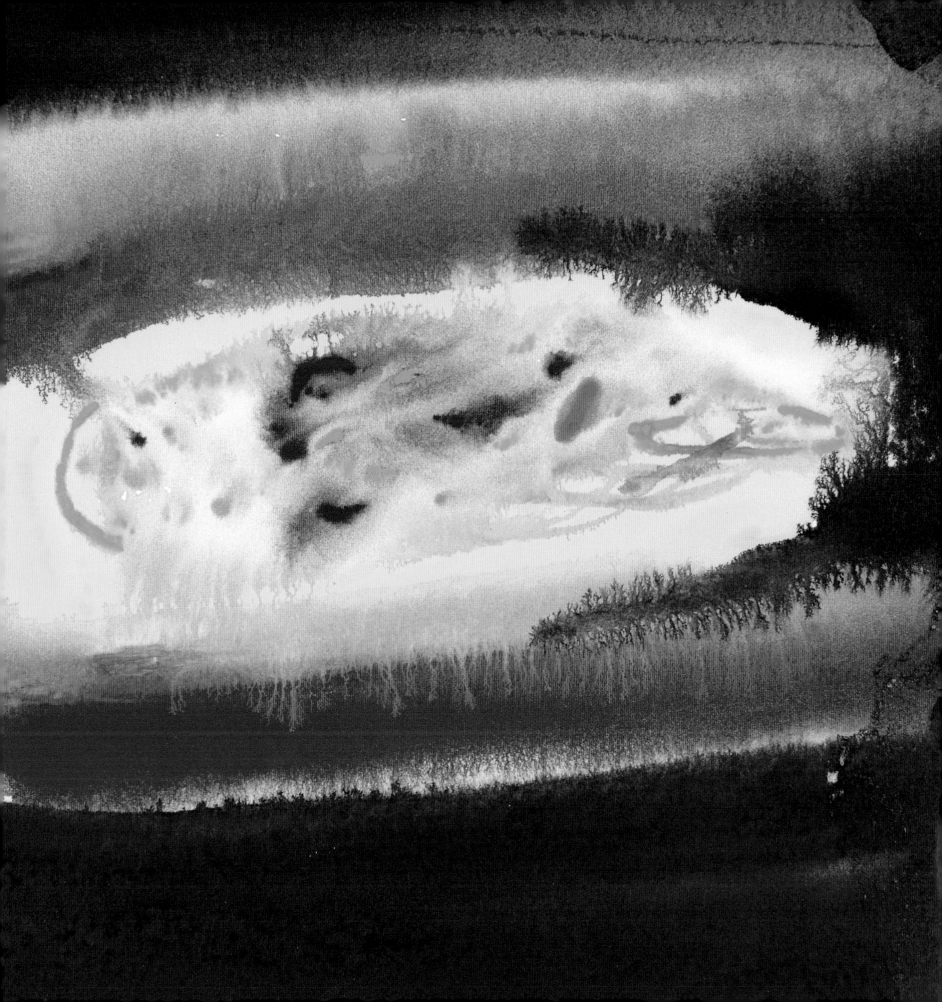

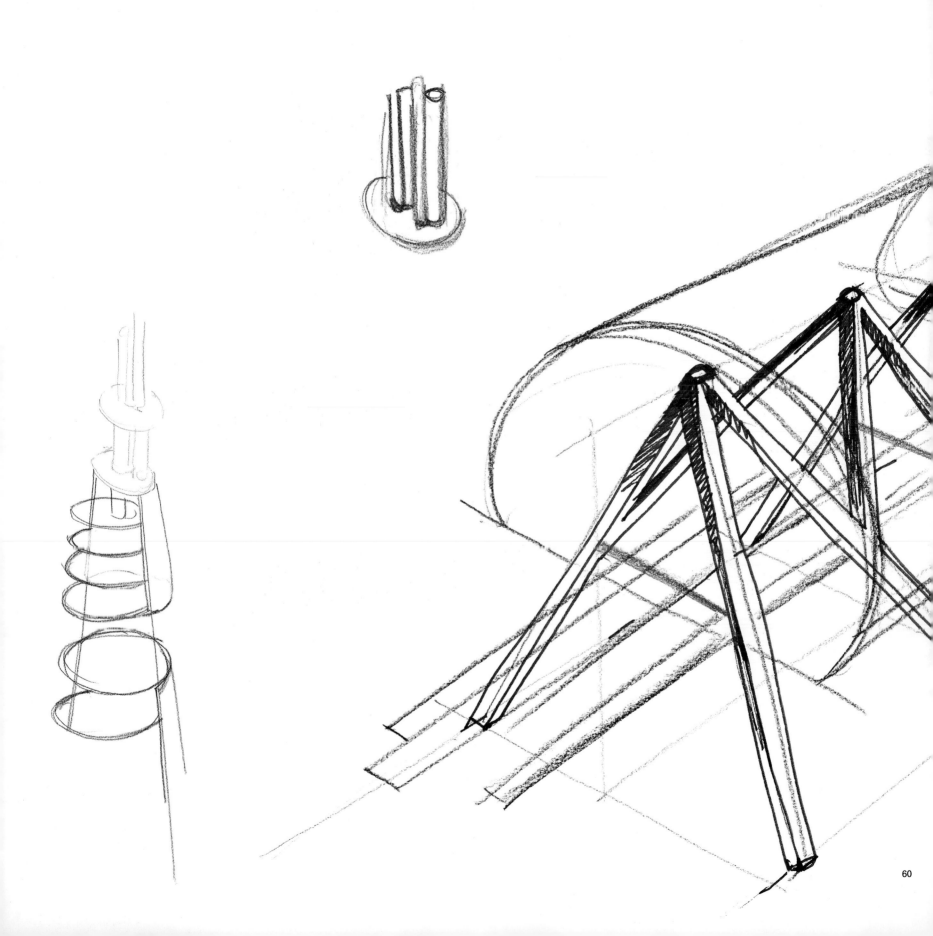

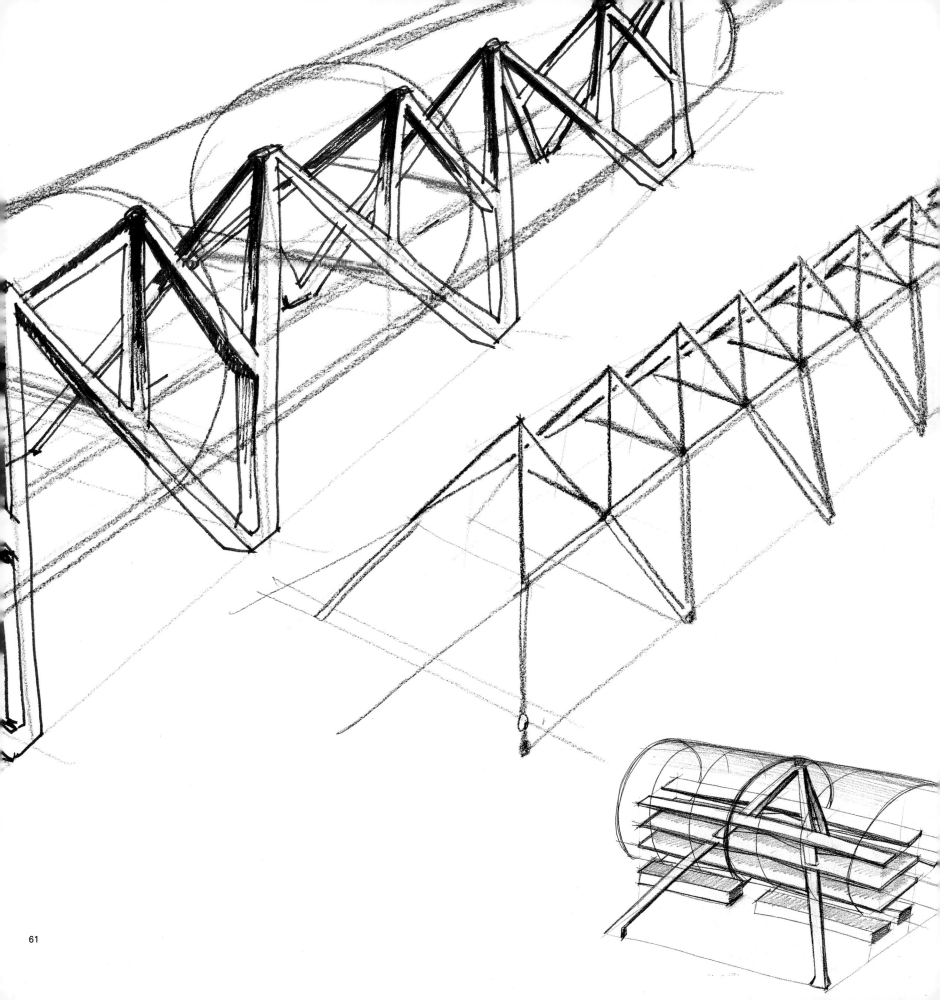

61

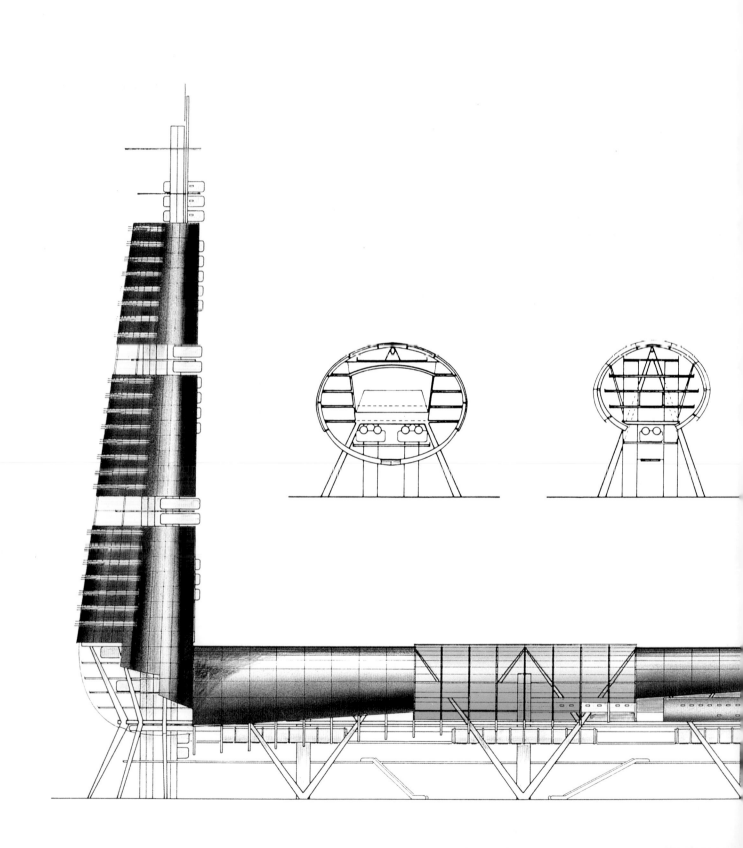

Daimler Benz Office, Conference Centre and Theatre Complex

This proposal applies the idea of progressive colonisation. Beneath the glossy black space of the building is a concrete frame structure with partial enclosure. Pre-fabricated-box accommodation slots into the concrete rack when it is needed.

The glass bank in the centre is the location of the theatre. To its left, next to the tower, is the conference centre. The tower contains office space and a clear, full-height, naturally lit atrium.

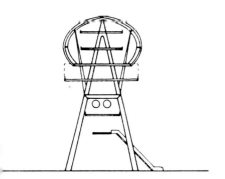

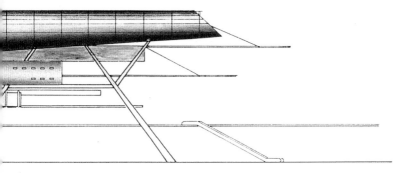

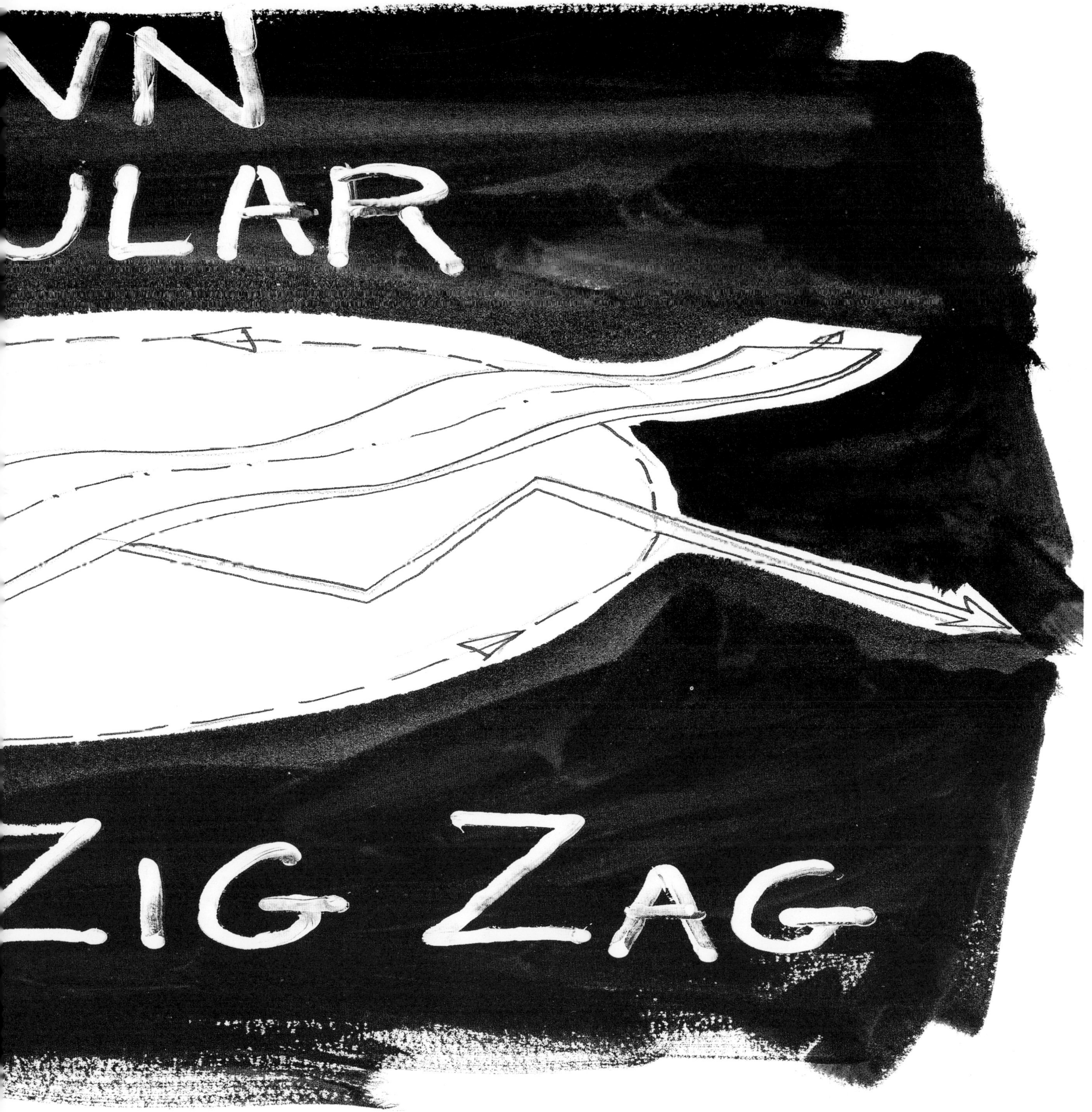
ULAR
ZIG ZAG

What is happening in Berlin? There is great confusion which has resulted in a return to conservative views and expectations mixed with nationalism. What *should* happen in Berlin? The city should take the unique opportunity it has to develop a test bed for a continuing experiment into urban and suburban life, forms and structures. With *uncertainty*: there is no guarantee that any proposal would work. Once this good principle is accepted there is no reliance on history. Dare you imagine it, let alone realise it? (Alsop: notebook entry, January 1992)

No guarantee

that the proposal would work We live with the disastrous failures of proposals *guaranteed to work*.

The principle of
uncertainty:
in Berlin above all it should be acknowledged that there are no certainties. They have crumbled all around: how many times, how many ways, in the memory of the century?

'*Form follows function*' encapsulates perfectly the modernist impulse to a purity of form, with nothing extraneous to it: buildings should match what is *predetermined* for them in terms of use. In the 1990s there is no certainty as to what will become the use of a given building. (In fact there never was.)

Alsop (*apropos* Marseille 1991) on the programme for practical working zones and other functional areas: '*For me this kind of programme has nothing to do with eternity. It must change.*' ('In fact, people can only tell you what they want on the basis of what they already know…'). Functions, and the designation of spaces for them, will change in unpredictable ways. Alsop regards this as fact and virtue: he works with that assumption; he takes delight in that assumption.

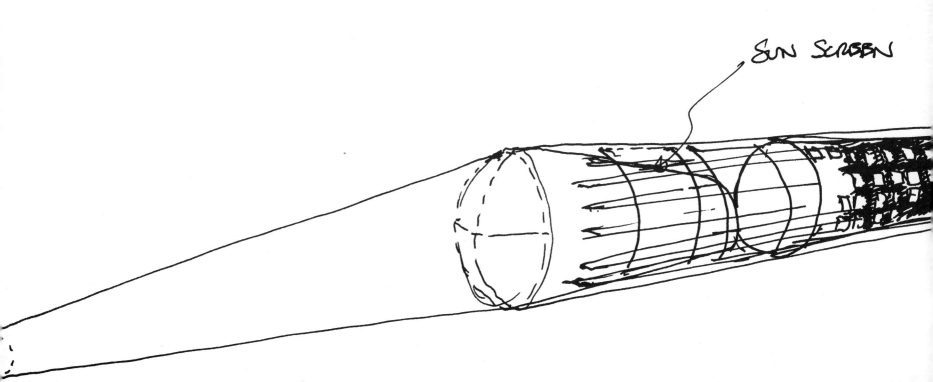

SUN SCREEN

Street of Dance
a film.

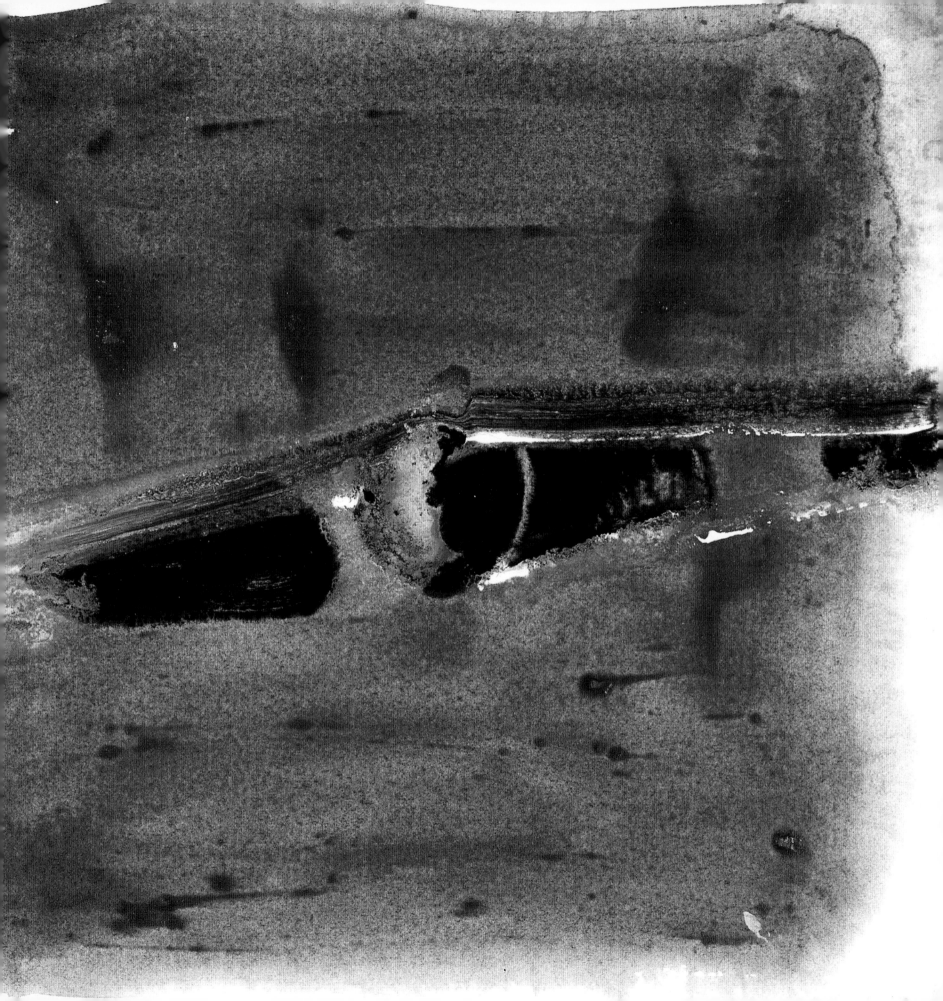

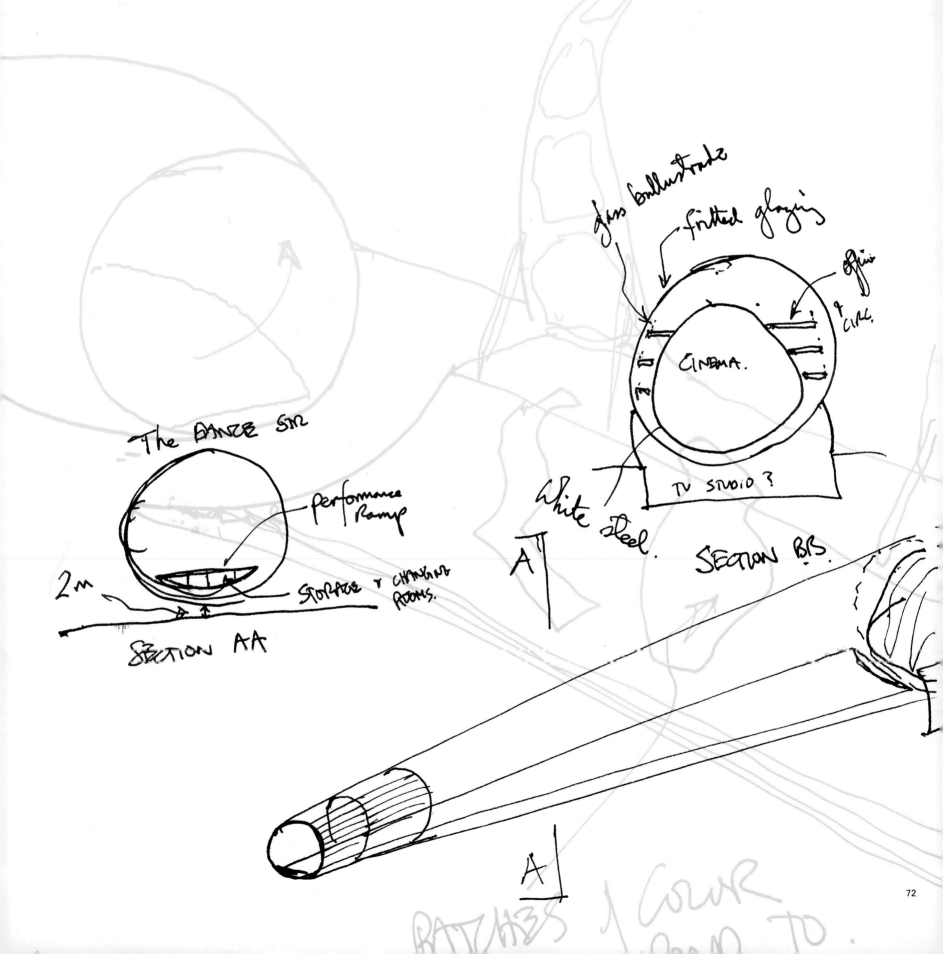

glass ballustrade

fritted glazing

offices
& circ.

CINEMA.

TV STUDIO ?

White steel.

SECTION BB.

A

The DANCE STR

performance
Ramp

2m

STORAGE + CHANGING
ROOMS.

SECTION AA

A

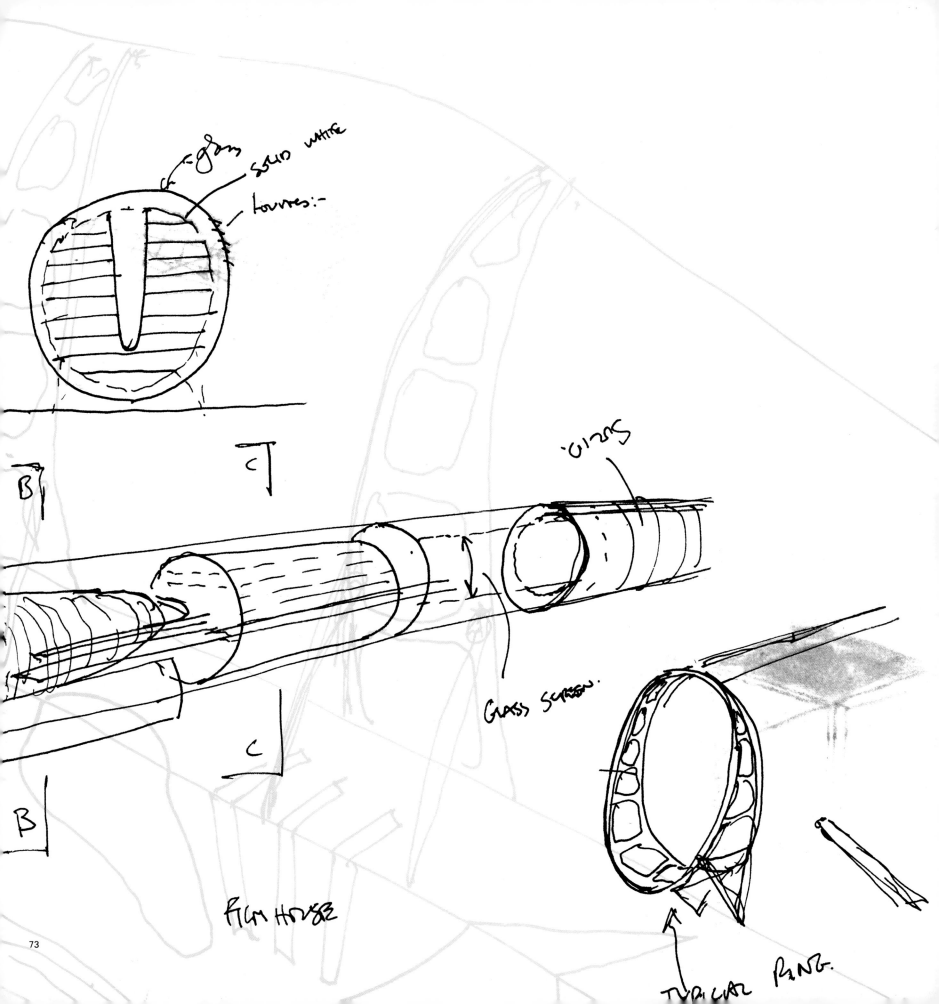

glass
SOLID WHITE
louvres:-

Ø125

glass screen.

B
C

C

B

FILM HOUSE

TYPICAL RING.

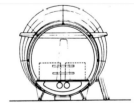

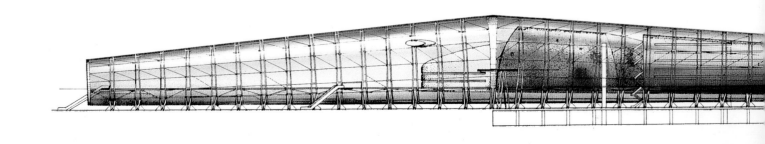

**Sony Filmhouse
Street of Dance**

The building consists of two truncated cones, joined mouth to mouth. The cone shells are supported by concrete rings, each of which is a looped ladder form, wider at the base than at the head. Accommodation is contained within amorphous blocks which are themselves enveloped in the glass double cone.

Occupying the shorter glass cone is the Street of Dance, a simple wide floor – both a thoroughfare and a performance area. Facilities housed in the floor allow adaptation for more formal presentations, but this would normally be an open forum. The longer cone contains the three-cinema complex and an office block. These are contained in amorphous concrete volumes, with strongly pigmented shells. The cinemas would house the Berlin Film Festival, at present without a permanent base.

The Potsdamer Platz end of the building houses a shopping centre. This section has solid plate-steel cladding. It connects to the Filmhouse across an open section of the cone, on elevated walkways.

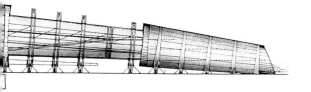

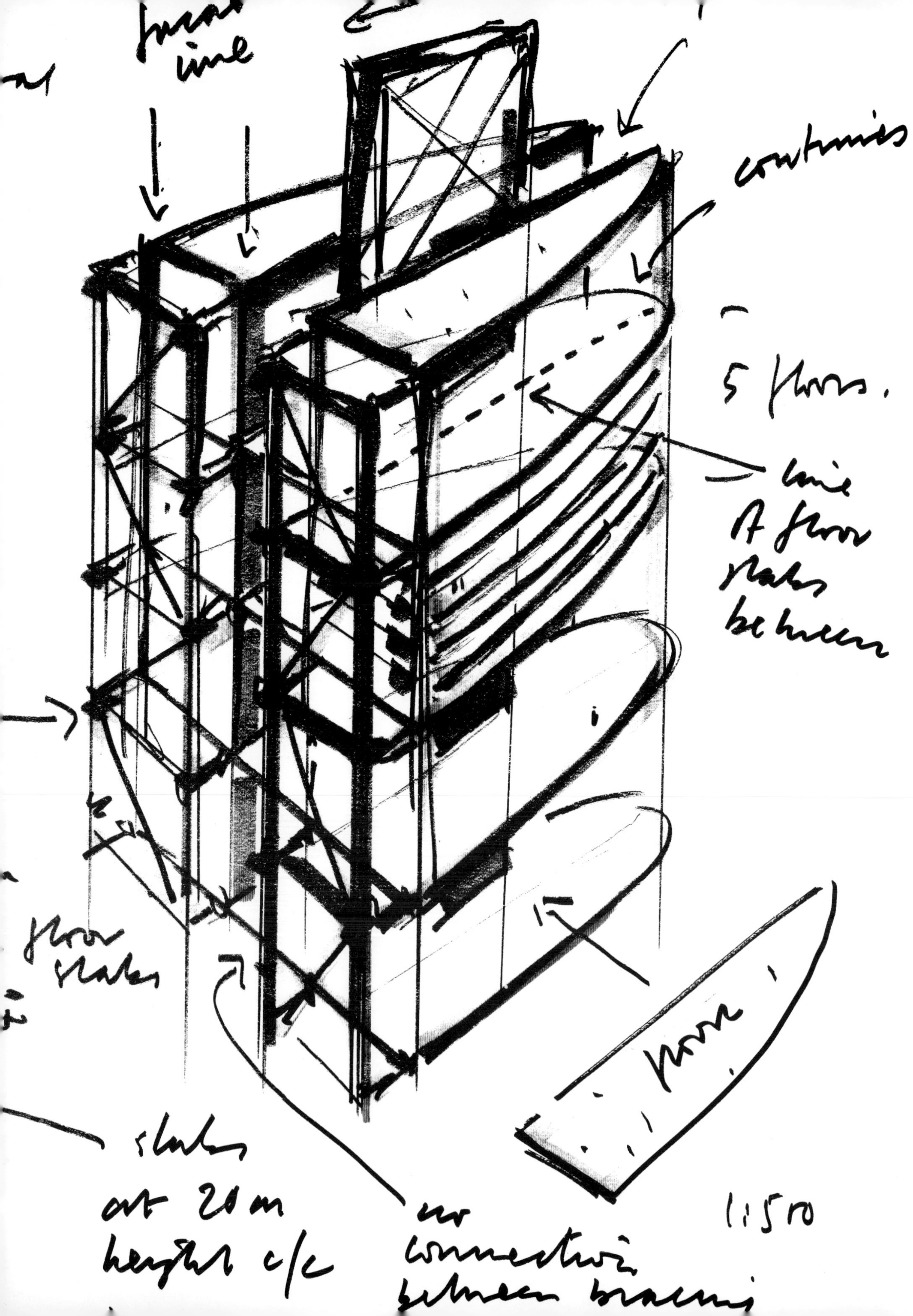

facade line

continues

5 floors.

line
if floor
slabs
between

floor slabs

slabs
at 20m
height c/c

no connection
between bracing

floor

1:500

Frederick Engels on Charles Fourier: 'Fourier takes the bourgeoisie, their inspired prophets before the Revolution, and their interested eulogists after it, at their own word. He lays bare remorselessly the material and moral misery of the bourgeois world. He confronts it with the earlier philosophers' dazzling promises of a society in which reason alone would rule, of a civilisation in which happiness should be universal, of an illimitable human perfectibility, and with the rose-coloured phraseology of the bourgeois ideologists of his time. He points out how everywhere the most pitiful reality corresponds with the most high sounding phrases, and he overwhelms this hopeless fiasco of phrases with his mordant irony.'

Berlin!
Berlin! Berlin knows better than any city in the world the ironies of history.

Mordant irony is the very mode of Berliner humour. They recognise rhetoric wherever it comes from. (JFK: 'I am a doughnut.')

Berlin knows better than any city in the world the ironies of history:
(Hitler hated Berlin: 'Just how little the Third Reich cared about Berlin's historical image can be seen by the fact that on January 30, 1937, at the beginning of the [700th] anniversary year, Hitler proclaimed his plan for a new Berlin, the notorious Speer plan, which envisaged a total rebuilding of the centre city and its conversion into a gigantic "Germania", the capital of the Thousand Year Reich. All through 1937, venerated buildings in the heart of Berlin were torn down (such as the Schlüterhaus, the Palais Schwerin, the

Ephraim Palais, the Krögel), destroying Berlin's historical substance at the very moment when one pretended to celebrate it.' – Gerhard Weiss)

Berlin does not need any more rhetoric: especially in its buildings.

No more Grand Manner: no more of the 'urbanism of dominion' for 'the staging of power.'

Berlin is a city saturated in the history of the twentieth century: its beauty is of the raw present. What the time demands is not theatrical spectacle (*no more Grand Manner!*) but an emphatically new modernism: not monuments and vistas, but a place *to be*. (To be = to change.)

Spectacularly *beautiful*, its colour unconstrained by monochromatic political and civic *gravitas*: a polychrome city centre! A paradox for the twenty-first century: a non-systematic non-prescriptive utopia (contra system/contra *phantasy*): not an attempt to think the impossibly *perfect* city centre, not a resuscitation of beautiful old solutions. Emphatically *not* an Haussmannian *embellissement stratégique*! (Haussmann was Hitler's favourite town planner.)

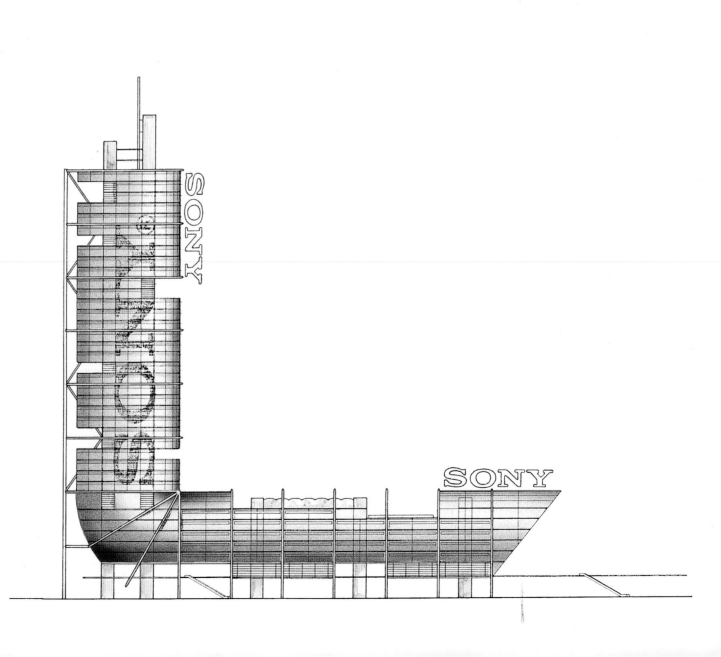

Sony Office Building

The tower houses head-quarters offices, the street level accommodates a department store, and leisure activities are located on the upper level of the street.

The tower is constructed around a traditional structural core. This makes it possible to raise the bulk of the tower far enough above the ground to let daylight penetrate fully beneath the building, allowing the floorscape to continue without interruption. The front face of the tower has a secondary frame structure which supports a full-height television display screen. The back 'edge' of the tower – the plan of which is again identical to the cross-section of the horizontal street element – is made up of multiple-height viewing bays, some of which are open to the air. The horizontal street is occupied by a a large department store, 25,000m² in area. A leisure complex is located along the ridge.

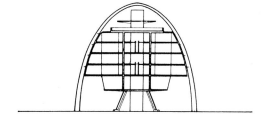

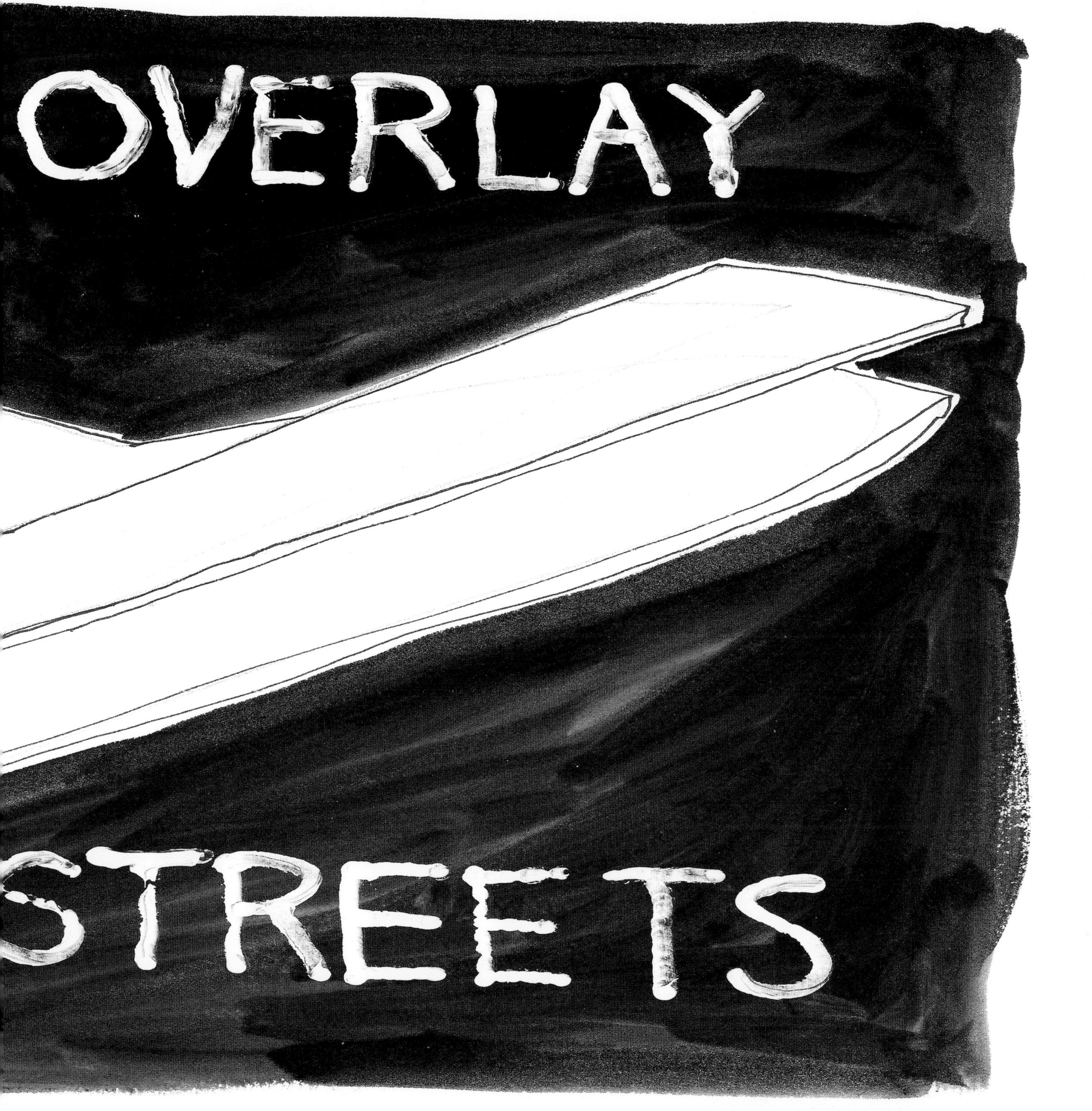
OVERLAY
STREETS

Construction plays the role of the unconscious.

Every epoch dreams its successor.

(Michelet quoted by Walter Benjamin)

Utopias are systematic: against the uncertainties contingent upon real social life they oppose an ideal order: to paraphrase a brilliant insight of Engels, they are 'formulations of disappointment'. They are alternative cities, set up in a 'no-place', they feel 'the need for compactness and permanence in opposing the world they reject' (Calvino). They are not dreams but projections, positive extrapolations from the negativities of painful experience. 'The more completely they are worked out in detail the more they drift off into pure phantasies.' Their potency is poetic; their effect is satiric. Their structures, as Benjamin recognised, are derived from the machine; relations within them are predictable and *according to plan*. Their value? – They 'enlarge the sphere of what we can imagine.' (Calvino)

'The politics in my work is not a reaction to events; it is an anticipation of events.' (McLean 1986)

architecture
imagines

architecture
dreams

architecture
constructs

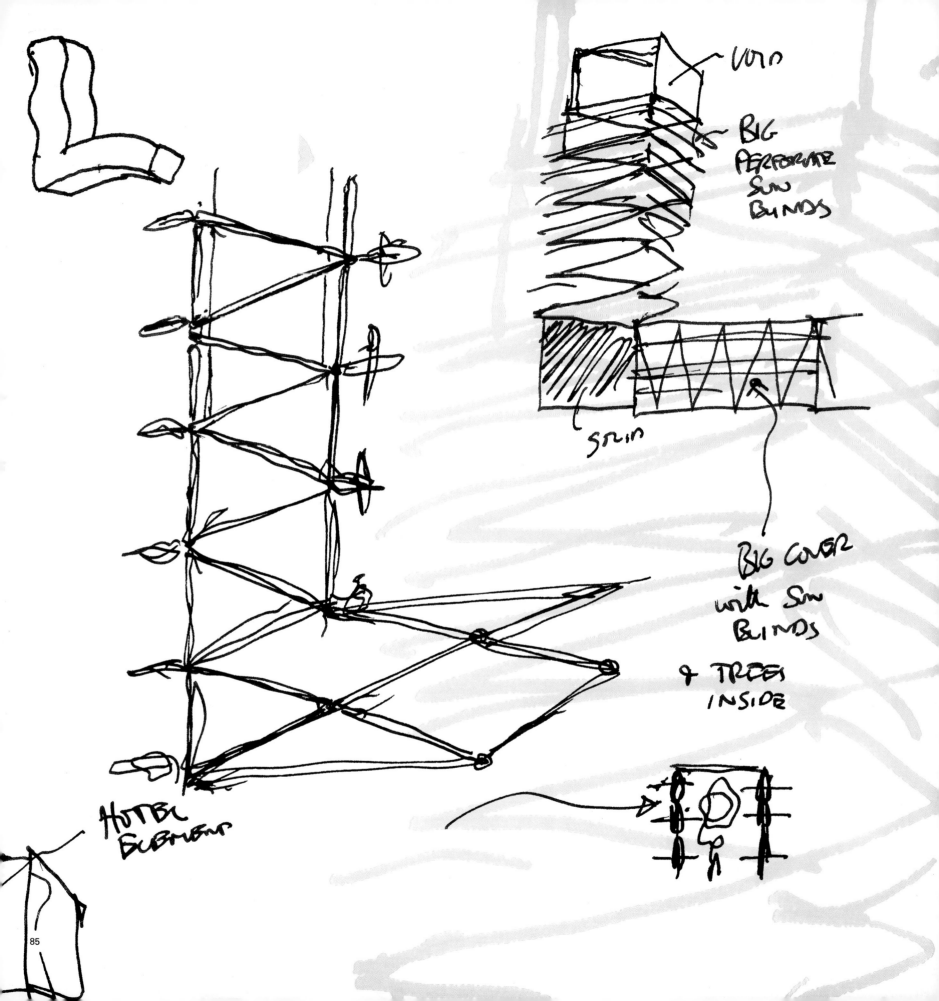

VOID

BIG
PERFORATE
SUN
BLINDS

SKIN

BIG COVER
with SUN
BLINDS
& TREES
INSIDE

HOTEL
ELEMENT

Sony Hotel

This is basically a glass box on a concrete slab and cone frame, with a secondary parasol structure supported by the zig-zag fascia bracing.

The building fuses with the existing listed building of the Hotel Esplanade – a well-known Berlin landmark and one of the few pre-war buildings to be retained on the site. The horizontal section of the new part of the hotel is a high, glass winter garden with full-size, mature trees growing inside.

Above this winter garden are four floors of accommodation. The whole structure is again raised, on legs, above the site to allow the floorscaping to continue underneath.

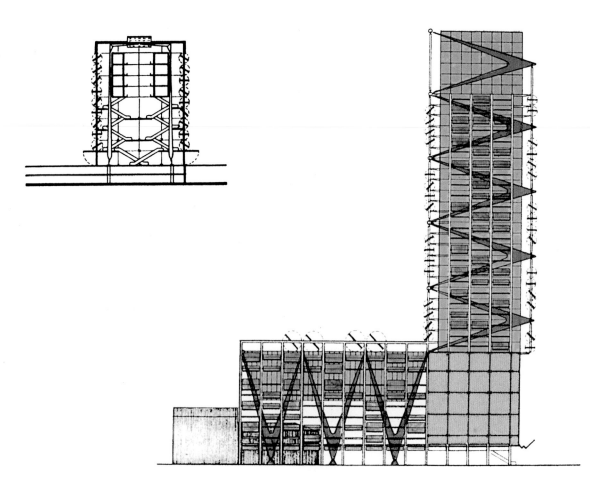

Wertheim Department Store

An interesting example of radical building development. The owners of the Wertheim site apparently intend to reconstruct their pre-war building exactly as it was prior to its destruction by bombing. This reconstruction is to be not just external, but internal as well, which must entail using nineteenth-century building techniques. By doing this they hope to avoid entanglement with the city planning officer because, technically, the building will not need planning consent. Thus, the drawing here is taken from the archives of the city of Berlin, but shows a proposal for the future of the site.

The building stands on the eastern edge of the competition site and has elevations onto Leipziger Strasse and, more significantly, onto three of the eight sides of Leipziger Platz itself. The rebuilding policy adopted by Wertheim is not discouraged by the city authorities. The ancient city grid and the sacred buffer level of 22 metres is much better preserved in the east city.

Alsop's decision was to draw a notional line across Leipziger Strasse – east of this the block form would be maintained. In effect this only takes up a small section of the competition area, but this line, following as it does the line of the recently removed Berlin Wall, was suggested to appeal to the historicism of some of the more conservative members of the city's adjudicating panel. The building proposed for the opposite side of the Leipziger Platz was a mirror image of Wertheim's store.

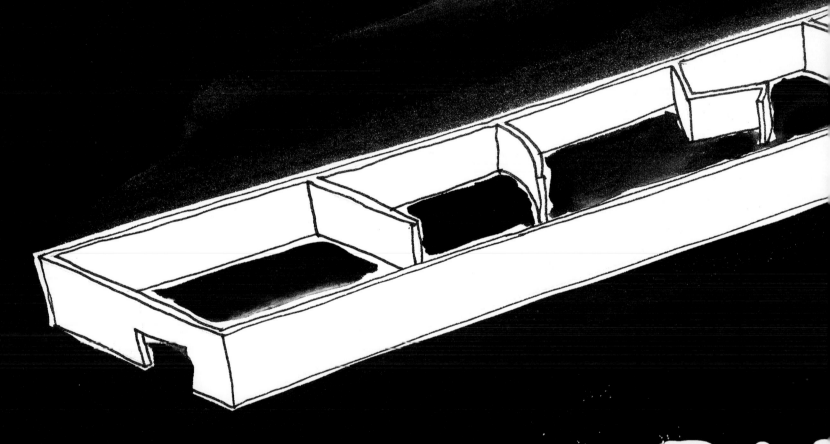

OF

LDINGS

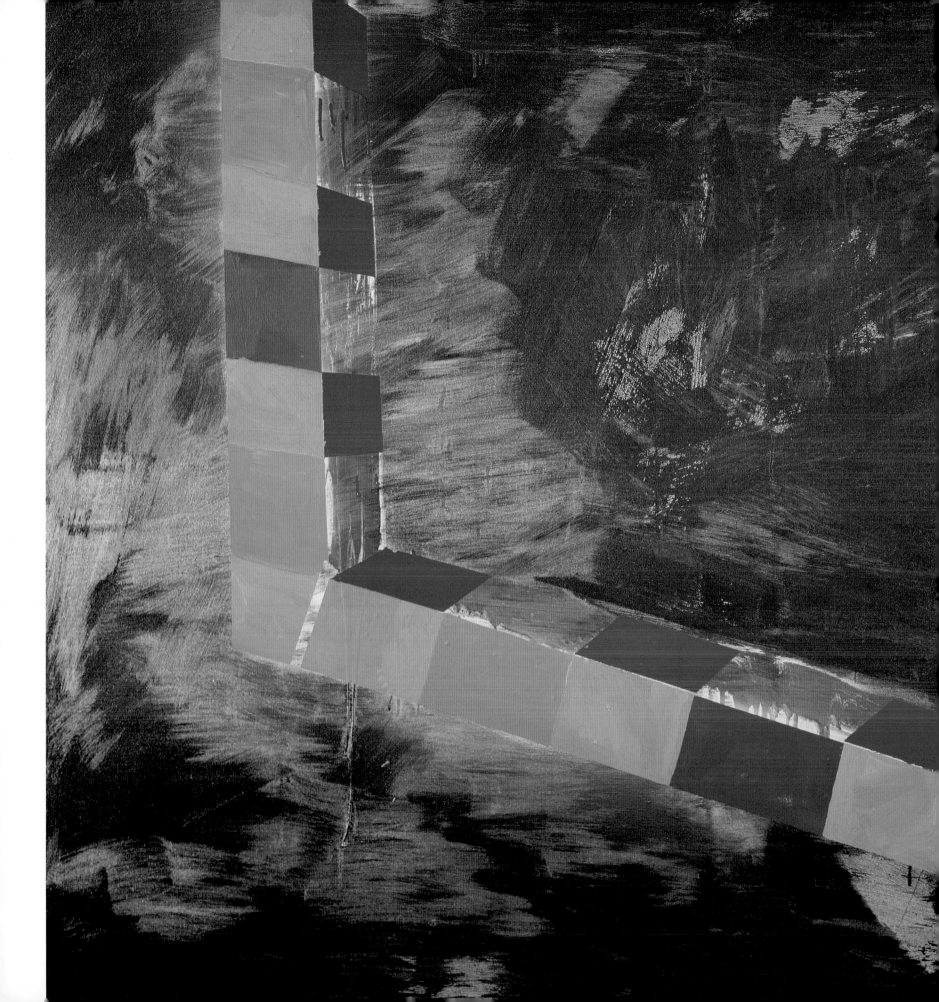

imagine

dream

construct

Re-think the platz/re-think the street/
re-think the buildings of the centre-city:
combine them. Imagine realistically.
Make it possible! It is possible.
Start with: *no plan*!

'Generate things that will have to be
discovered: This is what we must do!'
(Alsop 1991)

'Dare you imagine it, let alone realise it?'
A non-systematic, non-prescriptive
utopia?

'I want to make very big works, whether
it is with architects or governments, there
is something I have to do which hasn't
been done yet.' (McLean 1981)

'Every epoch dreams its successor.'

To Dream is to Create: a surrealist
watchword may be surprisingly apt. Cf.
Walter Benjamin: 'The utilisation of
dream-elements in waking is the
text-book example of dialectical thought.
Hence dialectical thought is the organ
of historical awakening. Every epoch not
only dreams the next, but while dreaming
impels it towards wakefulness.'

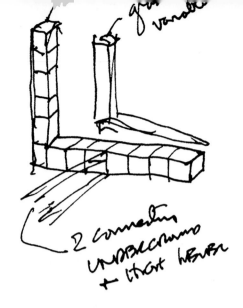

2 connecting underground
+ light house

BUILDING TWO

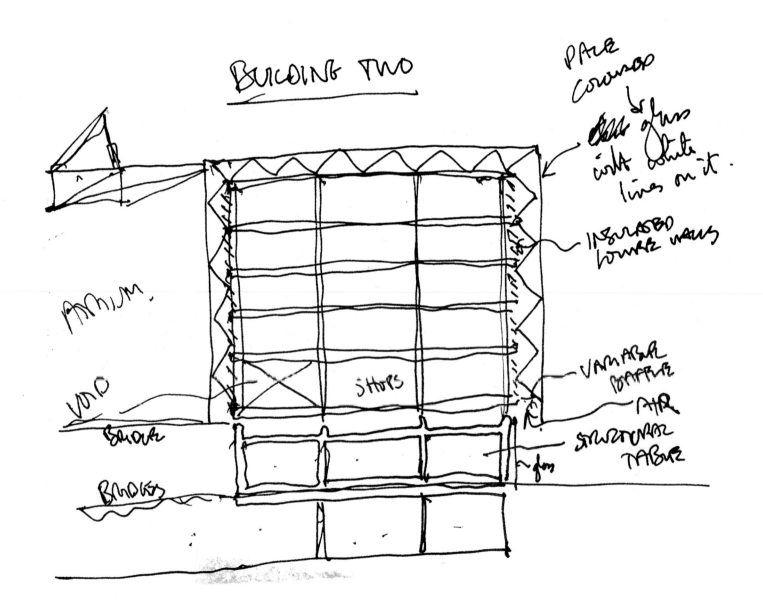

PALE COLOURED

glass with white lines on it.

INSULATED LOUVRE WALLS

ATRIUM.

VOID

BALCONY

BRIDGES

SHOPS

VARIABLE BAFFLE

AIR

STRUCTURAL TABLE

glass

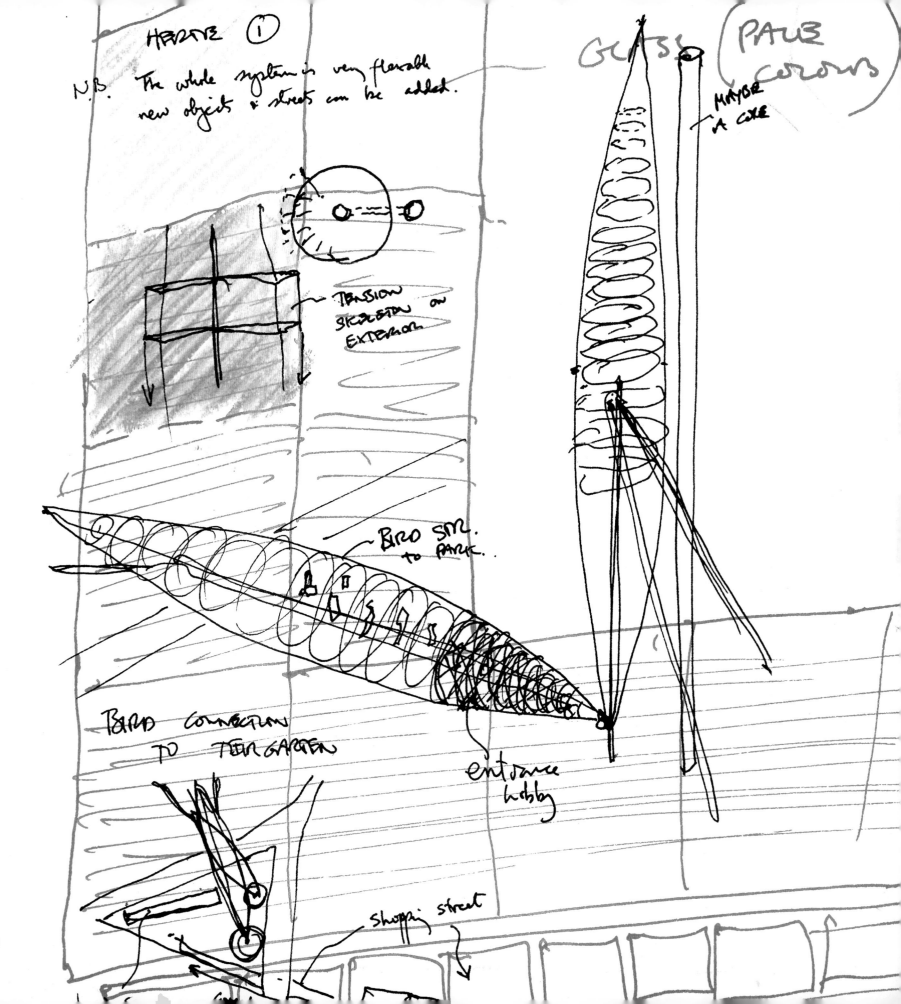

HERITE ①

N.B. The whole system is very flexible
new objects & streets can be added.

GLASS (PALE COLOURS)

MAYBE A CORE

TENSION SKELETON on EXTERIOR

BIRD STR. TO PARK.

BIRD CONNECTION TO TIERGARTEN

entrance lobby

Shopping street

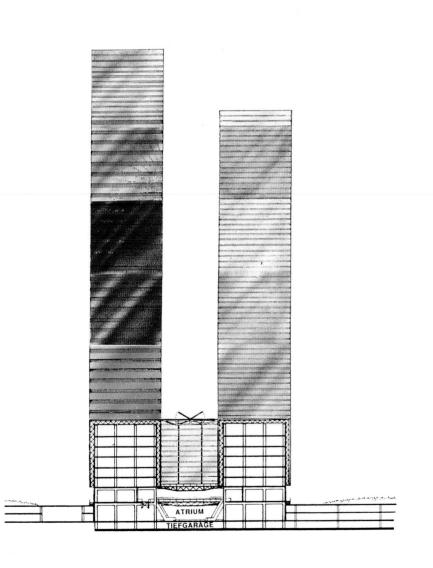

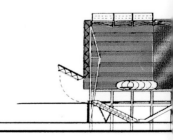

ATRIUM

TIEFGARAGE

Hertie Building

Again the landowners' mixed use development brief (offices, shops, housing) is brought together in a single structure, this time of twin towers, parallel street sections, and a large covered atrium connecting them. The taller tower containing the Hertie headquarters offices is a concrete-frame structure with bands of stone enamelled steel and glass around it. Steel panels are brightly coloured in blocks, as is the street connected to the tower. The street contains Hertie's own big shopping complex.

The shorter tower contains housing – a concrete frame with clear glazing, a climatic buffer zone, and then the outer skin of tinted float glass, giving the tower a coloured block appearance but with less saturated colour than the tall tower.

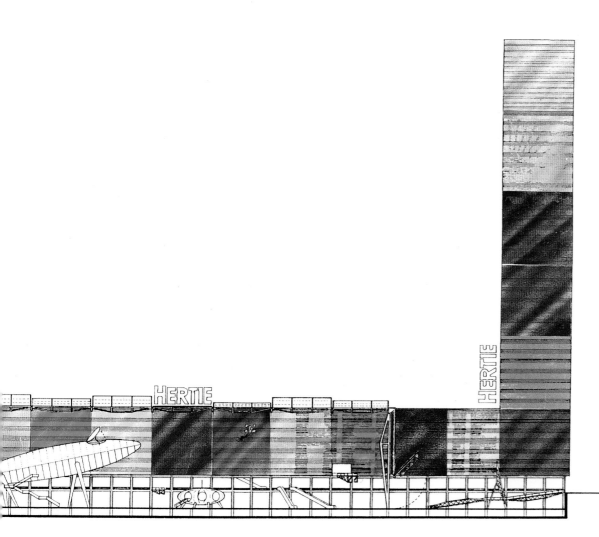

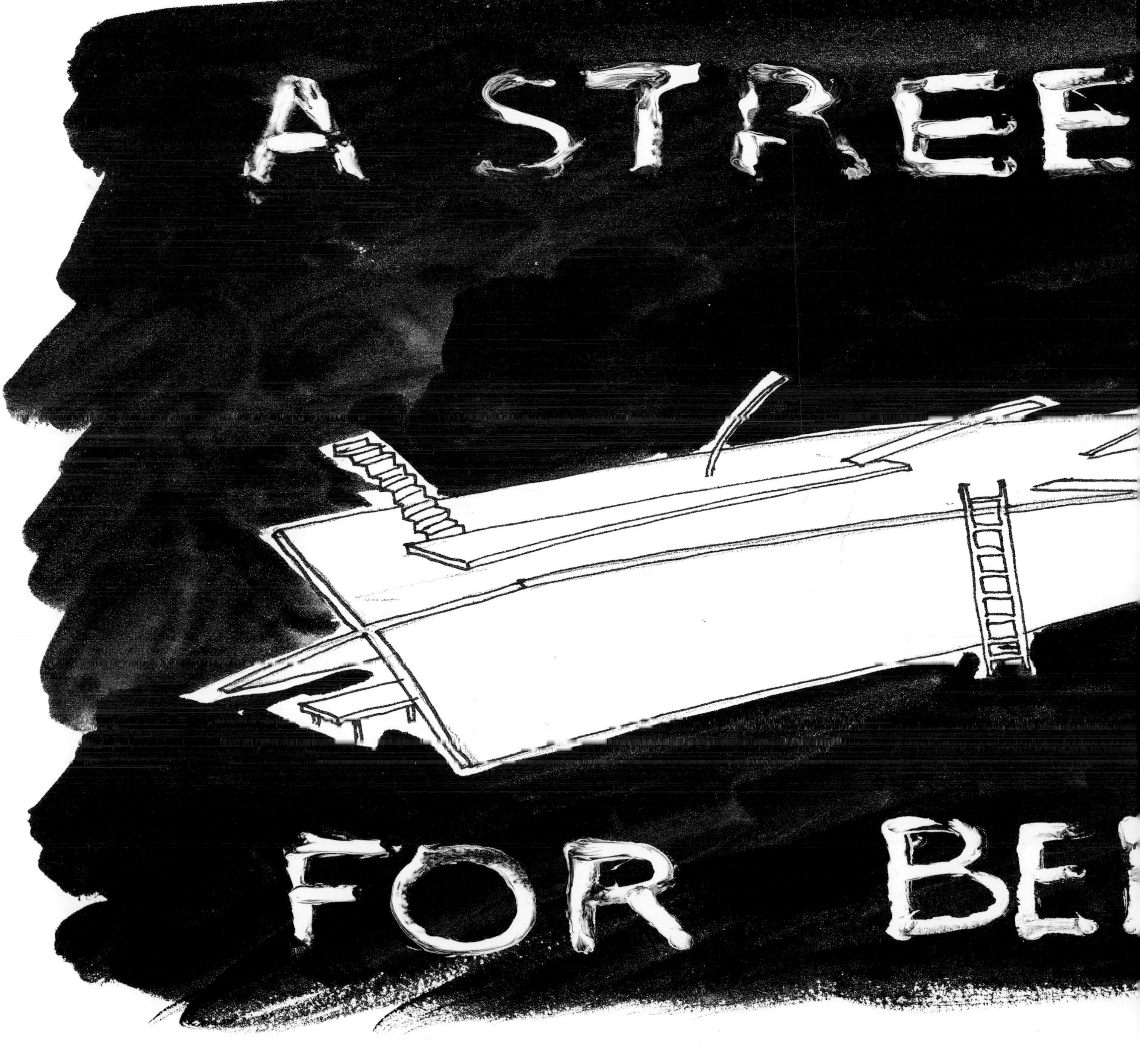
A STREE
FOR BE

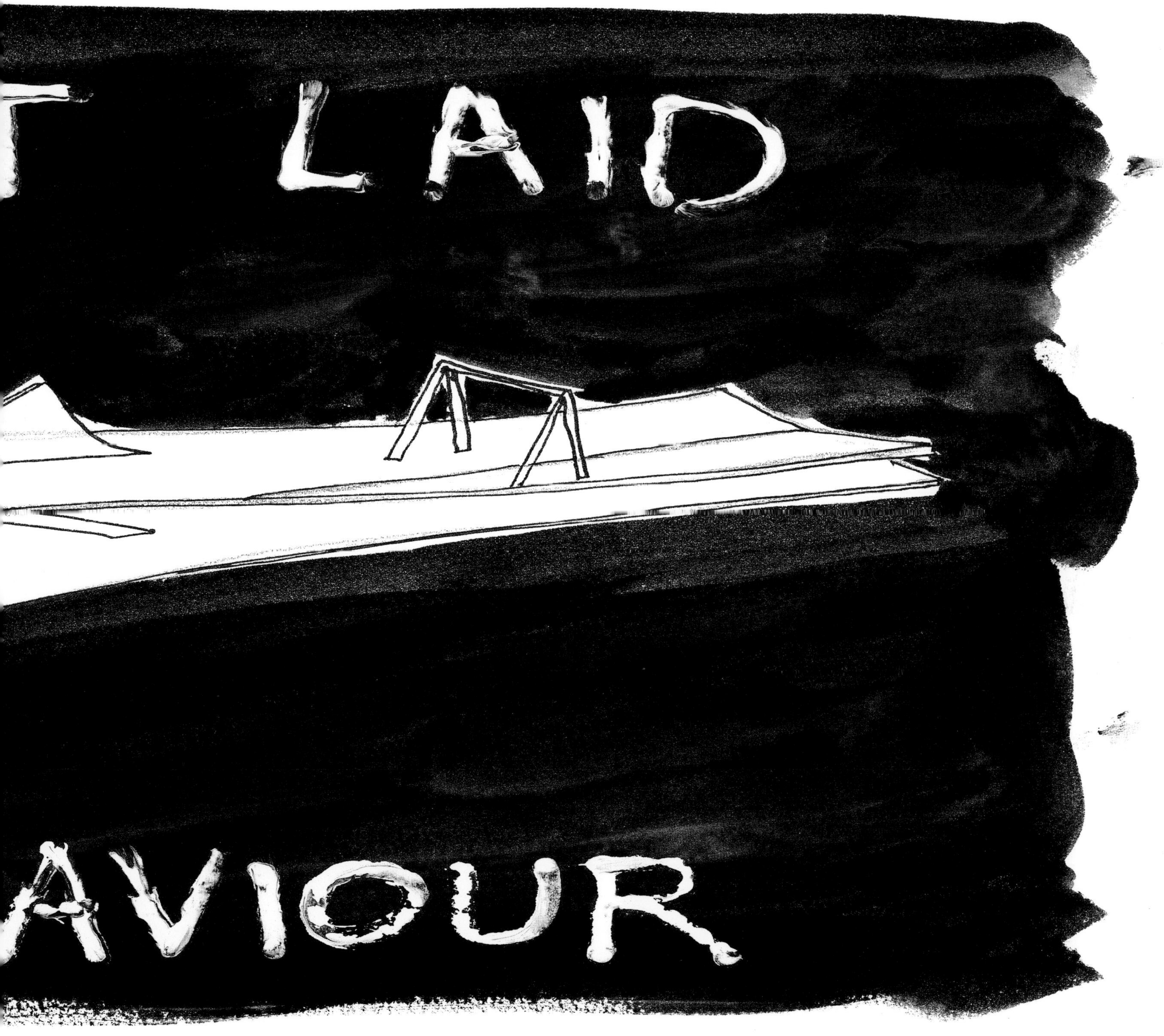
LAID
AVIOUR

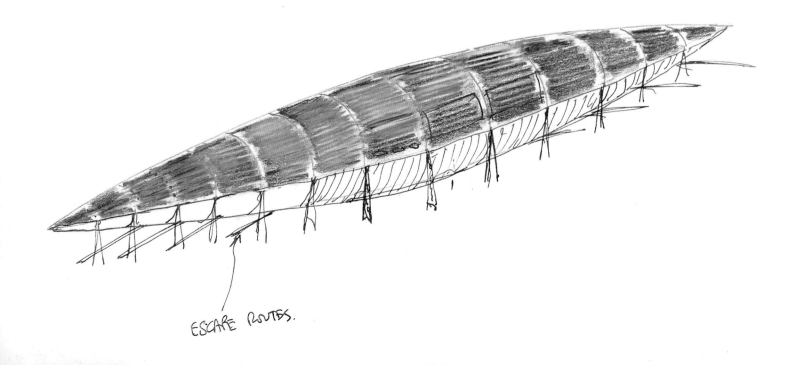

ESCAPE ROUTES.

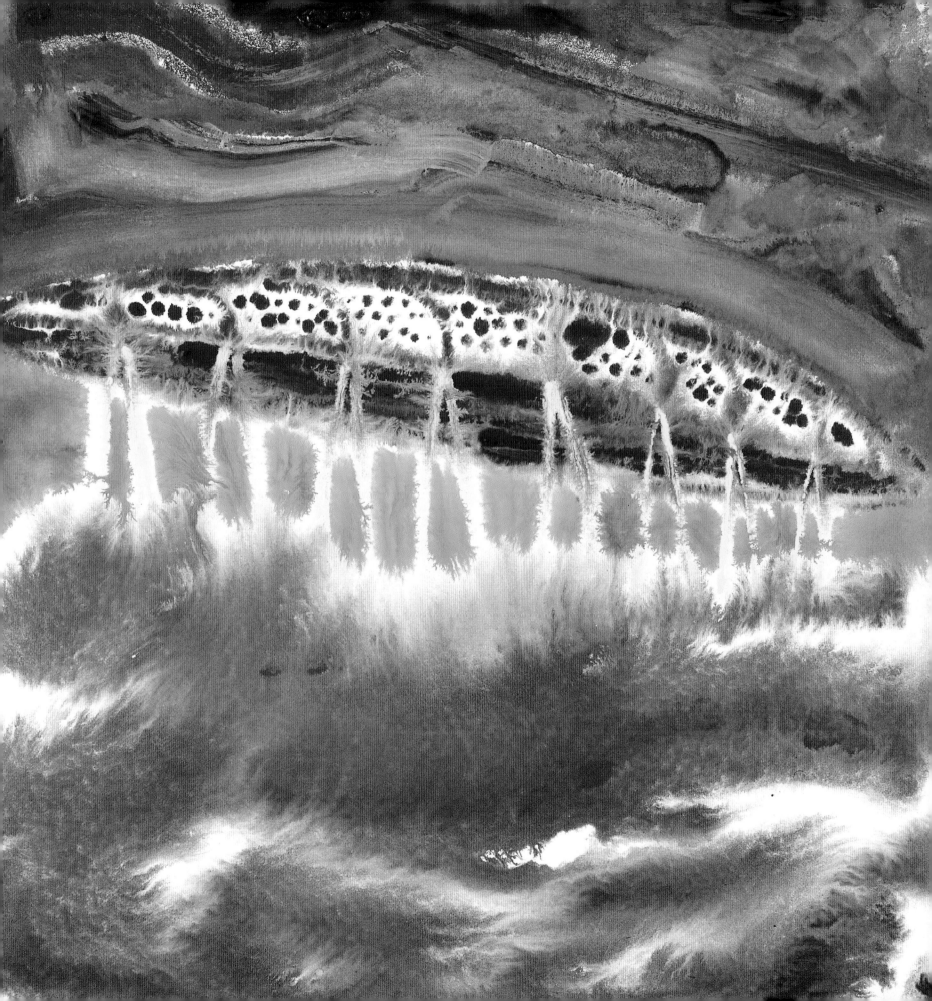

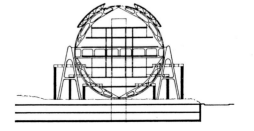

Ebertstrasse Hotel and Offices

This is one of the buildings designed for sites not owned by the large commercial concerns. The land below the site is still partly in the ownership of the city of Berlin and the former East German asset-disposal agencies.

The building contains an hotel in the upper half and offices in the lower half. The upper shell is clad in dull grey lead or terne-coated steel. The lower half is fully glazed. Punched openings with glass infills into the hotel rooms are protected from excessive solar gain by roving parasol screens that traverse, on tracks, from one side of the upper shell to the other.

The hotel necessitates a large number of escape stairs. These are used as additional structural bracing to keep the building poised on its belly.

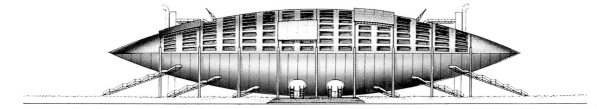

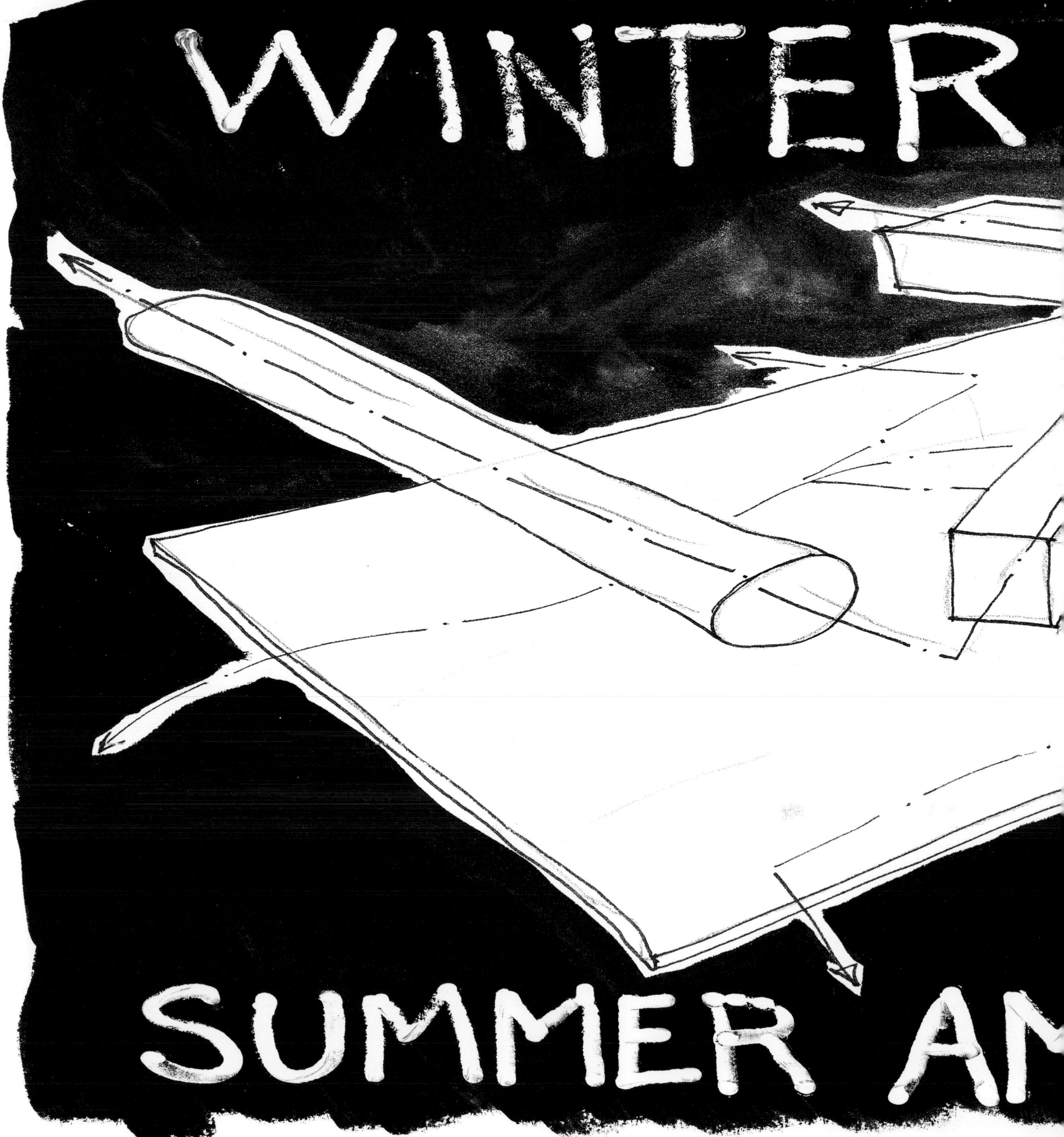
WINTER
SUMMER AN

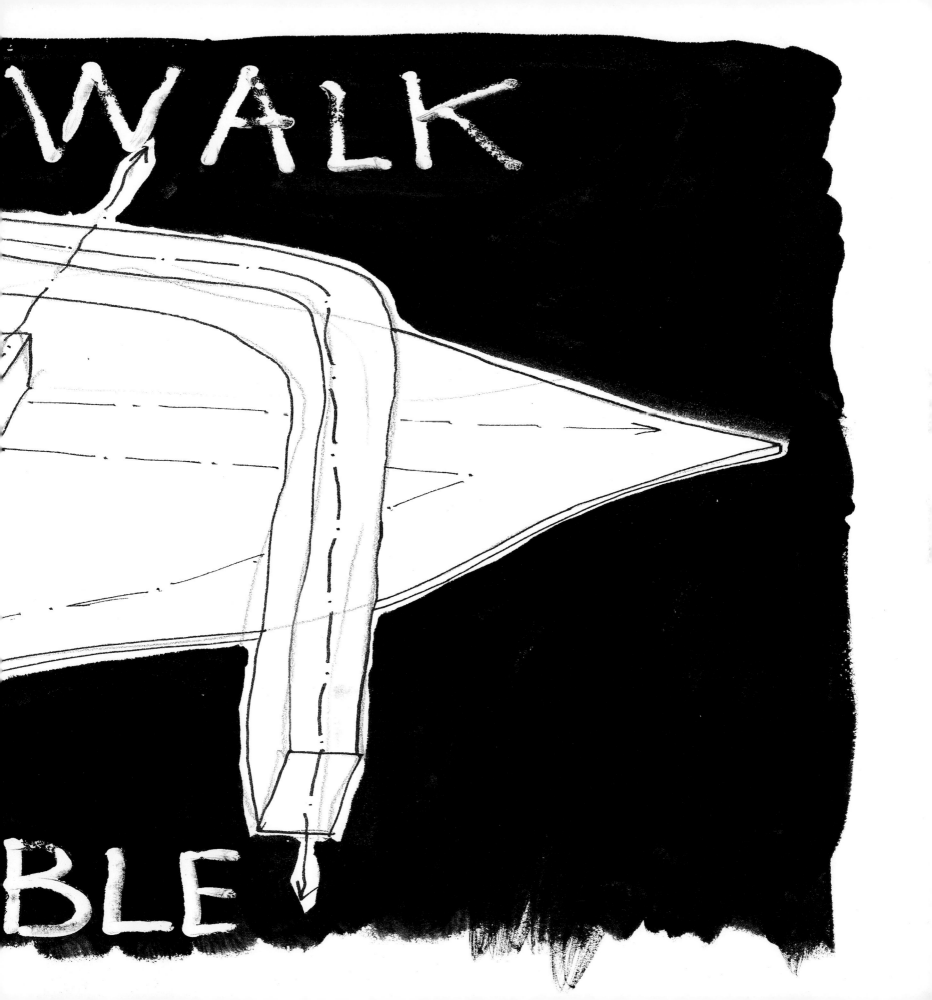

Art transforms the heart of the city:
the city centre becomes *a work*.
(Alsop: 'What I learned as an artist
helps me to design architecture.'
André Breton: 'A work of art is only of
value in as much as it is subjected to the
vibrations of the reflexes of the future.'
McLean: 'Art is trying to make things
that may be able to effect a change.')

The streets respond to the weather:
'No need to shut everything in!' But
awareness of the day's turning light and
the seasons' great cycle need not be
uncomfortable: 'you must open up the
construction process, create opportunities
for the city to become more pleasant,
more complex…' (Alsop)

'… the city was now a landscape, now
a room.'

A place *to be*.

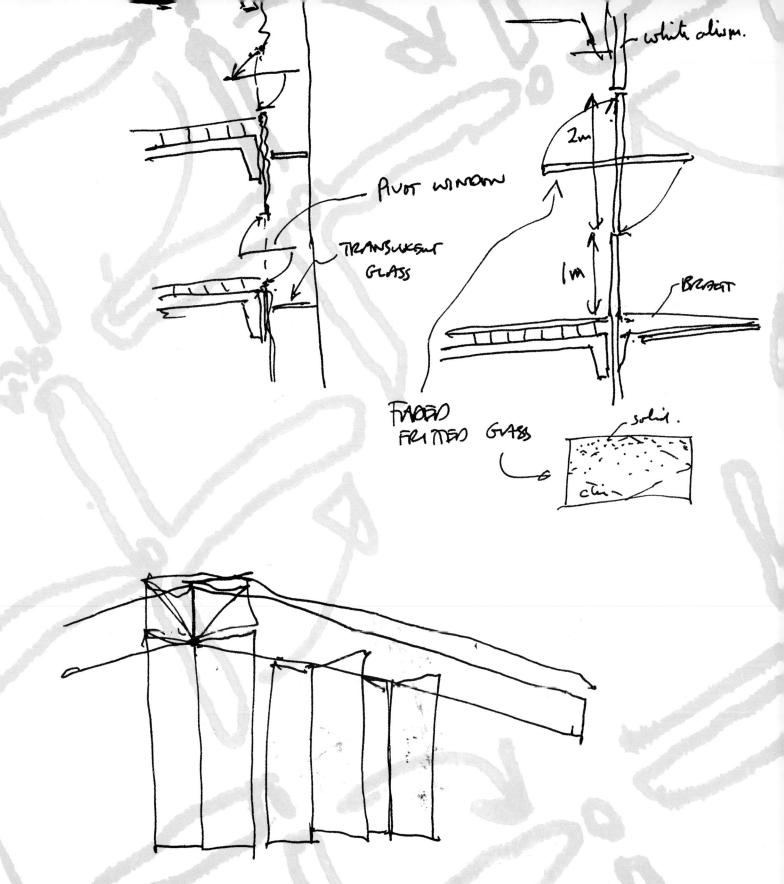

white alum.

PIVOT WINDOW

TRANSLUCENT GLASS

2m

1m

BRACKET

FADED FRITTED GLASS

solid.

clear.

PALACE of ART

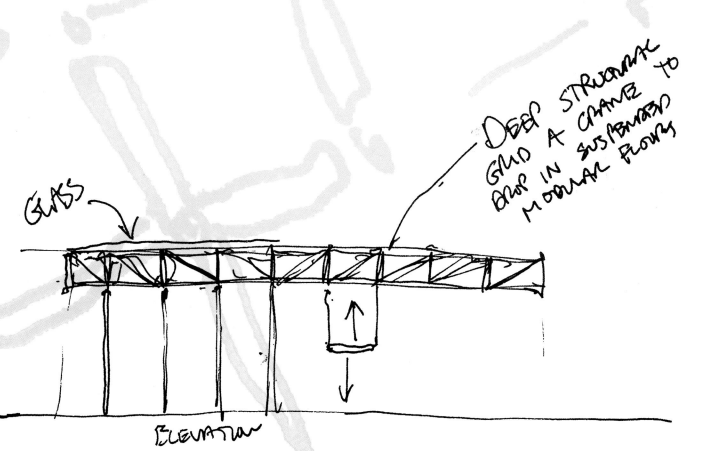

PLAN

ELEVATION

GLASS

DEEP STRUCTURAL GRID A CHANCE TO DROP IN SUSTAINED MODULAR FLOORS

POTSDAMER PLATZ

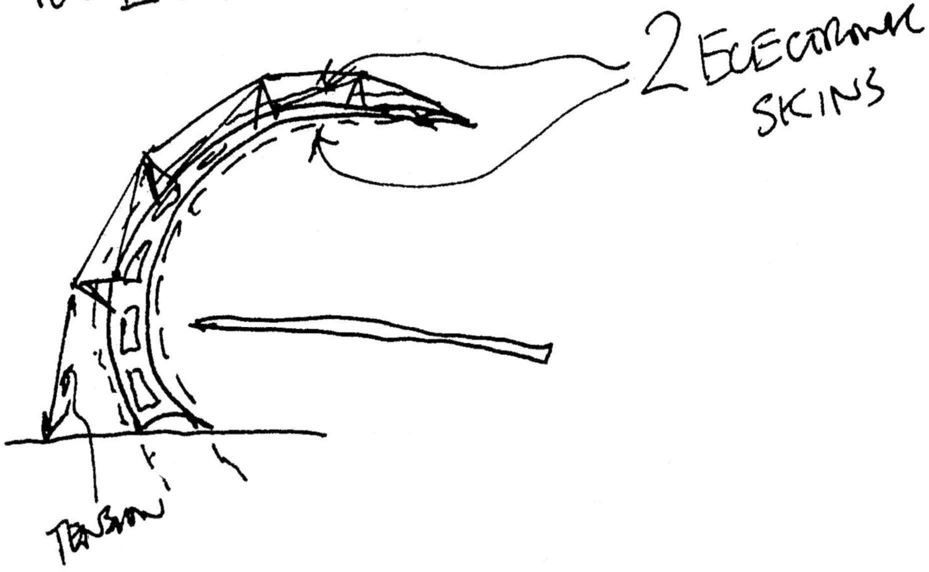

2 ELECTRONIC SKINS

TENSION

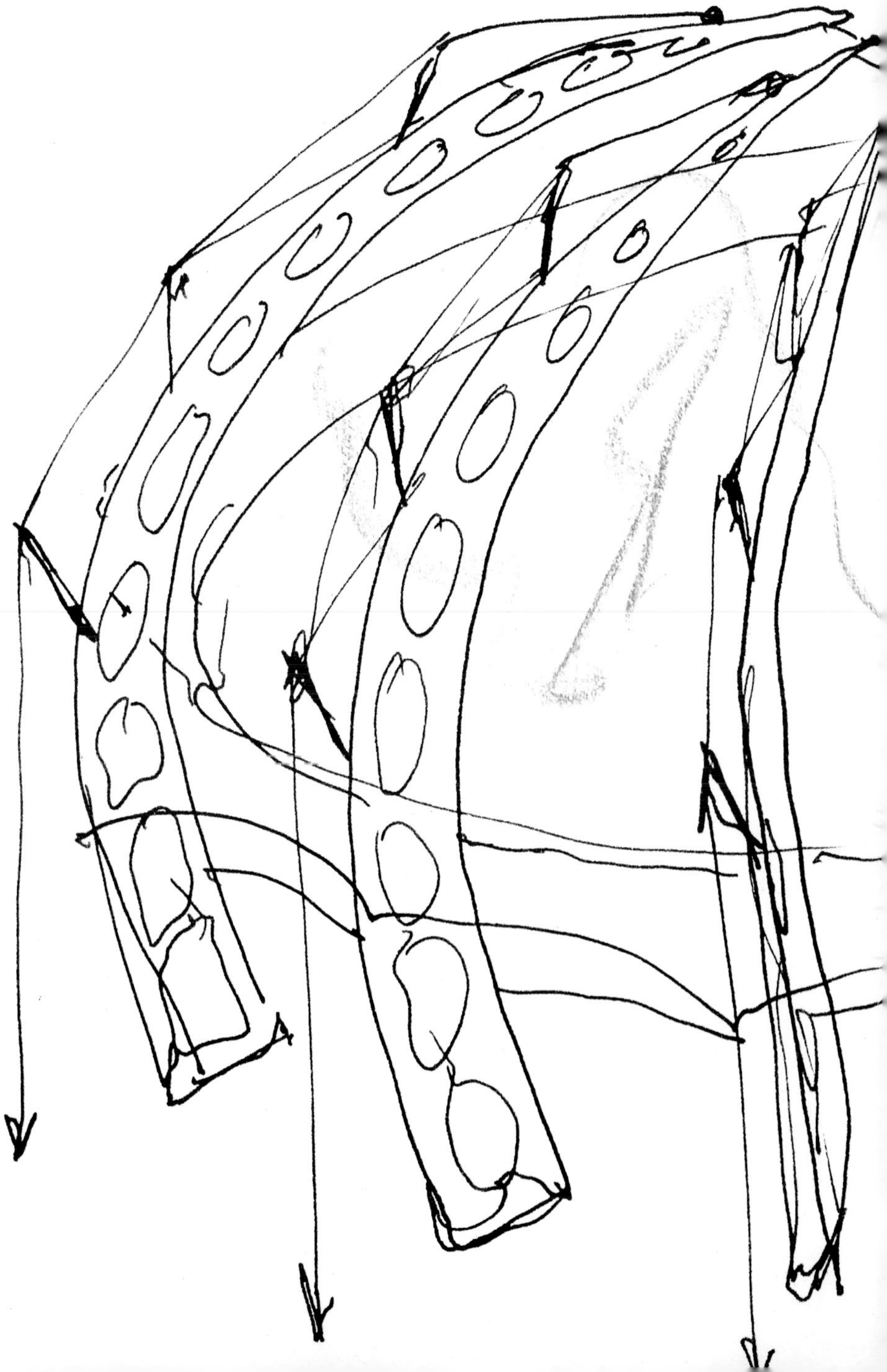

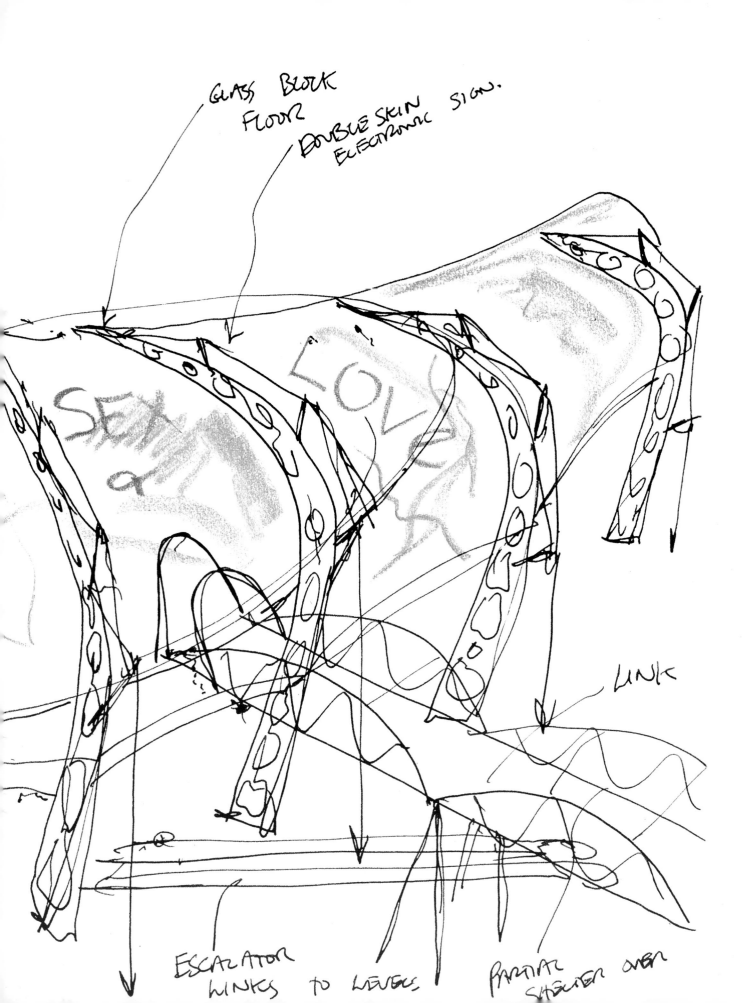

GLASS BLOCK
FLOOR

DOUBLE SKIN
ELECTRONIC SIGN.

LINK

ESCALATOR
LINKS TO LEVELS

PARTIAL
SHELTER OVER

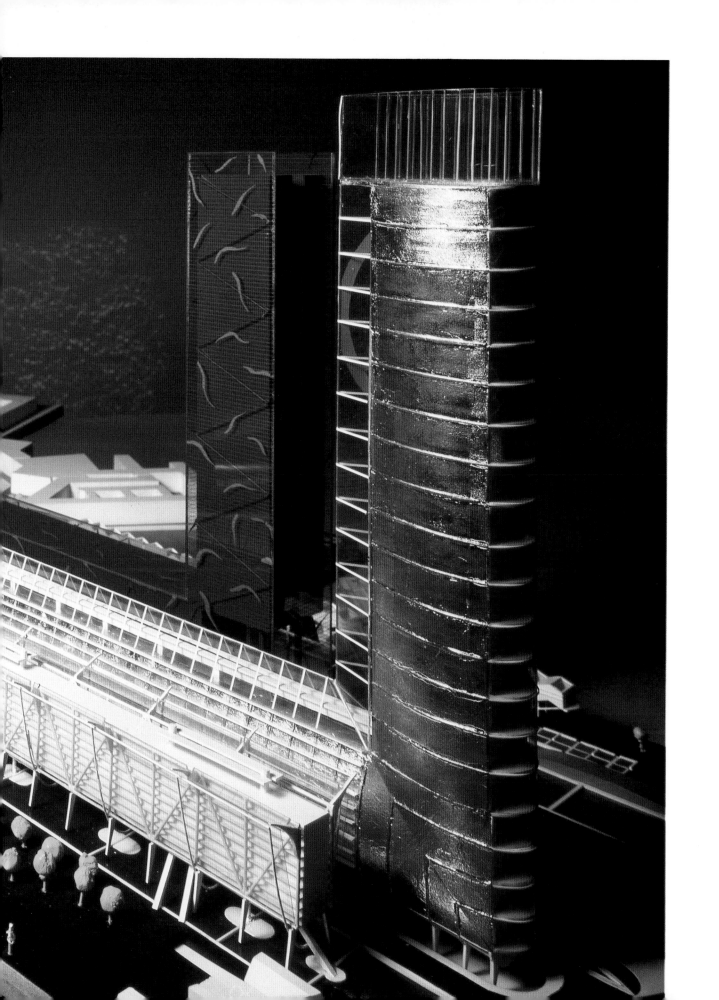

the squares are
married From the launch pad into the radial
streets: according to desire or necessity,
play or business, to walk, look, shop,
dance, work, pose, entertain, be
entertained. Each street accessible,
different: a brilliant dream of great
arcades transposed from the last to the
next century. A stupendously beautiful
Galleria! (Remembering Mengoni's
Milan masterpiece also marries two
great *piazze*.)

From a nineteenth century illustrated
Paris guidebook: 'These arcades, a new
contrivance of industrial luxury, are
glass-covered, marble-floored passages
through entire blocks of houses … On
both sides of these passages, which
obtain their light from above, there are
arrayed the most elegant shops, so that
such an arcade is a city, indeed a
world, in miniature.' (Quoted by
Benjamin.)

STR of
REMEMBERANCE
BERLIN

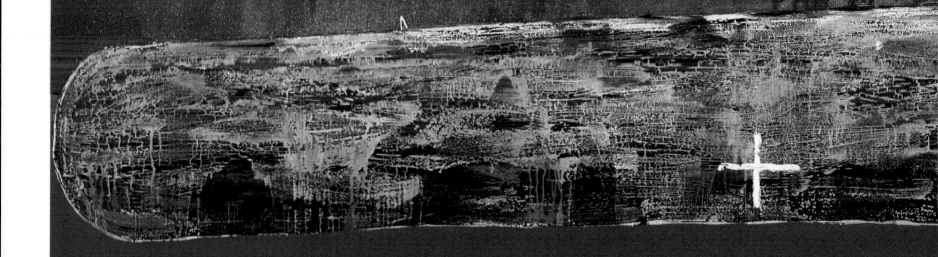

Frederick Kiesler:

**Form does not follow function,
function follows vision.
Vision follows reality. Instead of
functional designs which try to
satisfy the demands of the
present, bio-technical designs
develop the demands of the
future.**

(NB: develop, not anticipate.)

Alsop:

'One should work here, of course, but
also be able to dream, imagine.'

Imagine

Dream

Construct

In November 1991 the result of the Potsdamer Platz/ Leipziger Platz competition was announced. The winning scheme, by Heinz Hilmer and Christoph Sattler, uses a traditional mix of avenues and boulevards with buildings meeting but not rising above Berlin's old 22-metre line. Alsop and Störmer's scheme was placed fourth.

Index

Principal sources for quotations in Texts: Le Corbusier, *Concerning Town Planning* (*Propos D'Urbanisme*), Paris 1946, London 1947. Italo Calvino, from three essays 'On Fourier' in *The Literature Machine*, Turin 1982, London 1987. Frederick Engels, *Socialism: Utopian and Scientific*, London 1892. Walter Benjamin, *Paris – The Capital of the Nineteenth Century*, Frankfurt 1955, London 1968. Gerhard Weiss, essay on Berlin anniversaries in *Berlin: Culture and Metropolis*, ed. Haxthausen and Suhr, Minnesota, 1991. Frederick Kiesler, 'Pseudo-Functionalism in Modern Architecture' in *Partisan Review* 16, New York, 1949. William Alsop: an interview with Marie Christine Lorioux (catalogue of Bordeaux exhibition); conversations with Mel Gooding, both 1991. The Grand Manner as the 'urbanism of power' is discussed in Spiro Kostof, *The City Shaped*, London 1991.